WITHDRAWN

SHARED SPACES

IMMIGRANT COMMUNITIES & ETHNIC MINORITIES IN THE UNITED STATES & CANADA: No. 63

ISSN 0749-5951

Series Editor: Robert J. Theodoratus
Department of Anthropology, Colorado State University

1. James G. Chadney. *The Sikhs of Vancouver.*
2. Paul Driben. *We Are Metis: The Ethnography of a Halfbreed Community in Northern Alberta.*
3. A. Michael Colfer. *Morality, Kindred, and Ethnic Boundary: A Study of the Oregon Old Believers.*
4. Nanciellen Davis. *Ethnicity and Ethnic Group Persistance in an Acadian Village in Maritime Canada.*
5. Juli Ellen Skansie. *Death Is for All: Death and Death-Related Beliefs of Rural Spanish-Americans.*
6. Robert Mark Kamen. *Growing Up Hasidic: Education and Socialization in the Bobover Hasidic Community.*
7. Liucija Baskauskas. *An Urban Enclave: Lithuanian Refugees in Los Angeles.*
8. Manuel Alers-Montalvo. *The Puerto Rican Migrants of New York City.*
9. Wayne Wheeler. *An Analysis of Social Change in a Swedish-Immigrant Community: The Case of Lindsborg, Kansas.*
10. Edwin B. Almirol. *Ethnic Identity and Social Negotiation: A Study of a Filipino Community in California.*
11. Stanford Neil Gerber. *Russkoya Celo: The Ethnography of a Russian-American Community.*
12. Peter Paul Jonitis. *The Acculturation of the Lithuanians of Chester, Pennsylvania.*
13. Irene Isabel Blea. *Bessemer: A Sociological Perspective of a Chicano Bario.*
14. Dorothy Ann Gilbert. *Recent Portuguese Immigrants to Fall River, Massachusetts: An Analysis of Relative Economic Success.*
15. Jeffrey Lynn Eighmy. *Mennonite Architecture: Diachronic Evidence for Rapid Diffusion in Rural Communities.*
16. Elizabeth Kathleen Briody. *Household Labor Patterns among Mexican Americans in South Texas: Buscando Trabajo Seguro.*
17. Karen L. S. Muir. *The Strongest Part of the Family: A Study of Lao Refugee Women in Columbus, Ohio.*
18. Judith A. Nagata. *Continuity and Change Among the Old Order Amish of Illinois.*
19. Mary G. Harris. *Cholas: Latino Girls and Gangs.*
20. Rebecca B. Aiken. *Montreal Chinese Property Ownership and Occupational Change, 1881–1981.*
21. Peter Vasiliadis. *Dangerous Truths: Interethnic Competition in a Northeastern Ontario Goldmining Community.*
22. Bruce La Brack. *The Sikhs of Northern California, 1904–1975: A Socio—Historical Study.*
23. Jenny K. Phillips. *Symbol, Myth, and Rhetoric: The Politics of Culture in an Armenian-American Population.*
24. Stacy G. H. Yap. *Gather Your Strength, Sisters: The Emerging Role of Chinese Women Community Workers.*
25. Phyllis Cancilla Martinelli. *Ethnicity In The Sunbelt: Italian-American Migrants in Scottsdale, Arizona.*
26. Dennis L. Nagi. *The Albanian-American Odyssey: A Pilot Study of the Albanian Community of Boston, Massachusetts.*
27. Shirley Ewart. *Cornish Mining Families of Grass Valley, California.*
28. Marilyn Preheim Rose. *On the Move: A Study of Migration and Ethnic Persistence among Mennonites from East Freeman, South Dakota.*
29. Richard H. Thompson. *Toronto's Chinatown: The Changing Social Organization of an Ethnic Community.*
30. Bernard Wong. *Patronage, Brokerage, Entrepreneurship and the Chinese Community of New York.*

SHARED SPACES
CONTEXTS OF INTERACTION
IN CHICAGO'S ETHNIC COMMUNITIES

Laurence Marshall Carucci
Michael Brown
Lynne Pettler

AMS Press
New York

Library of Congress Cataloging-in-Publication Data

Carucci, Laurence Marshall, 1949-
  Shared spaces / Laurence M. Carucci, Michael Brown, Lynne
Pettler.

     p. cm. — (Immigrant communities & ethnic minorities in the
United States & Canada ; 63)
  Bibliography: p.
  Includes index.
  ISBN 0-404-19473-7
     1. Chicago (Ill.)—Ethnic relations. 2. Ethnicity—Illinois—
Chicago. 3. Ethnology—Illinois—Chicago. I. Brown, Michael.
II. Pettler, Lynne. III. Title. IV. Series.
F548.9.A1C37 1989
305.8'00977311—dc19   89-31161
                                                                CIP

All AMS books are printed on acid-free paper that meets
the guidelines for performance and durability of the Com-
mittee on Production Guidelines for Book Longevity of the
Council on Library Resources.

AMS PRESS
56 East 13th Street
New York, N.Y. 10003, U.S.A.

MANUFACTURED IN THE UNITED STATES OF AMERICA

for
Vera and Larry
Laura and Amy
James, Jonathan, and Alma
whose guidance, patience, and understanding
help to mold our lives

CONTENTS

Page

PREFACE xi

INTRODUCTION xv

I

ANALYZING ACTIONS: PROXEMICS IN
        PERSPECTIVE 1

METHODOLOGICAL CONSIDERATIONS 30

II

ETHNOGRAPHIC SKETCHES 43

III

ANALYSIS AND COMPARISON OF ETHNIC
        INTERACTIONS 158

IV

FUTURE DIRECTIONS: RE-READING
        EDWARD SAPIR 229

GLOSSARY 239

ENDNOTES 242

BIBLIOGRAPHY 247

INDEX 253

The language of the body . . . is incomparably more ambiguous and more overdetermined than the most overdetermined uses of ordinary language.

Pierre Bourdieu, *Outline of a Theory of Practice*

Preface

Research for the current study was conducted fifteen years ago in several ethnic neighborhoods of Chicago. Our plans at the time were limited. We wanted to discover more about ethnicity, and we hoped to unravel a few questions that had been raised about cultural interaction styles. Both of those objectives were accomplished. But in spite of the fact that our subsequent paths have taken each of us in somewhat different directions, we have all discovered interested others who continue to ask about our study, and several who have eagerly encouraged us to make the material available to a wider audience. Indeed, while modes of investigating social interaction have become significantly more sophisticated in the intervening years, there is still a gap that is filled by this study. Thus, without the possibility of reconvening in the same neighborhoods to witness perduring patterns and changing interaction styles, we present the results of our study in largely unaltered and unadulterated form. Each of us might make significant changes in the text as a part of our own rethinking of interpersonal relationships, but the value of the original rests in what it is able to tell us about ethnic differences, and those figures are inalterable.

At the time, our choice of setting was doubly motivated: it was made primarily on the pragmatic grounds that all three of the researchers were graduate students at The University of Chicago, but, perhaps more importantly, it was inspired by a common interest in the diversity of the city's ethnic communities. As newly arrived residents of the city, we were categorized as "westerners" by local residents (a label that classified Chicago folks as much as it did us). Still, we wanted to discover if ethnic distinctiveness was purely a cultural category -- a way Chicago could claim to be a huge, complex city like New York -- or if ethnicity was also manifest in styles of social interaction. The study we designed could answer those questions. And what better way could be envisioned to carry out such a comparison than to do our work in neighborhood bars -- an obvious institutional setting in which ethnic identities are defined and elaborated? As the study progressed, though, we were faced with a question of how to discern interaction patterns that were group specific, in a statistical sense, from those that were context dependent. Our work in ethnic churches, a significantly contrastive setting, helped address this problem. As can be seen, however, the question of how the significance of an action relates to the units of analysis was never really solved. Our questions about situation specific significance led us to consider alternate settings but, in the end, the very methodology that allowed us to prove that ethnic differences existed, also placed a constraint upon what we could say these differences meant to those involved.

Beginning in relatively uncharted territory, we utilized the framework of proxemics proposed by Edward T. Hall as a comparative analytic tool. Naively, we hoped the coding method would give us a relatively unbiased method for recording non-verbal interactions. As shall become apparent, however, the method structured the information in several ways. The framework that allowed us to make certain types of intra-ethnic and inter-group comparisons, also prevented us from answering many questions about context-dependent significance. None-the-less, as much can be learned from the constraints of method as from analytic correlations. The ethnographic sketches in Chapter II were conceived and given birth in an attempt to reunite method and analysis. A number of recent studies had focussed on social interaction, but our work was designed to apply an anthropological method, participant observation, to interpersonal encounters in ethnic communities. Our very first attempts to observe interactions in ethnic bars made it eminently apparent that "just being there" had significant effects on how people acted, and we try to monitor these effects in the ethnographic sketches. Nonetheless, our imposition was always on a particular ethnic group's native ground -- quite a different situation than the unfamiliar setting where "informants" are "placed" in a laboratory (cf., Watson 1970). The participant observer approach can neither allow us to imply that the results are universally valid for certain ethnic groups nor that they are totally representative of the particular communities in question. The results are situation specific; they represent various sets of permissible actions in the contexts in which they were constituted, but in no sense do they exhaust the total range of valid encounter styles utilized by a particular ethnic group. One message we hope to convey in this book is that it is impossible to speak of an "ethnic interaction style" without talking about a "range of permitted actions". And, in order to know what each action signifier "means", it must be referenced to a particular culturally-defined event -- a stage (Goffman 1959) or arena (Turner 1974) -- and a specific interactive circumstance. The ethnographic sketches allow the reader to occupy a seat beside the ethnographers as a vicarious participant who shares some of our impressions and impositions.

The presentation has been divided into sections on theory and methodology, ethnographic sketches and maps of the settings, data analysis, and conclusions. We have attempted to separate research and analysis, and to allow the reader to be able to use each section to reflect upon the others and come to other interpretations that may not have been apparent to the researchers. Each section depends upon the others, though the order of their presentation does not reflect the manner in which one thought led to a subsequent critique or conclusion. The format we have selected requires that certain conceptual elements be repeated in various places. We hope these repetitions will not be a burden for our readers.

There are a number of people who contributed in significant ways to this work and a great deal of thanks and of credit goes to them. Bert Hozelitz and Sol Tax encouraged us to pursue this topic from its inception. Susan Fisher assisted in the early phases of the research and helped us "punch in" information collected during the first three months of the project. Norman McQuown and Starkey Duncan gave us critiques of early drafts, and Michael Silverstein and John Wiorkowski provided sound advice as we analyzed the material and worked our way through several drafts. Karl Heider, and Thomas Sebeok encouraged us to make this material readily available. Our editor, Robert J. Theodoratus, also provided valuable comments and suggestions. Mrs. Vera Carucci typed an early draft of the work and offered suggestions on later drafts, and Terri Wolfgram and Diane Furhman helped type recent drafts. Jack Gilchrist assisted with transfers from computer to computer and from disk to final copy.

Finally, we would like to thank Mary, Laura, Amy, James, Jonathan and Alma who listened, learned, and gave us their patient attention and love when the need was greatest.

Introduction

A person's nationality, David Schneider tells us, is structurally similar to kinship (Schneider, 1969). That is, it is a cultural phenomena with boundaries established by birth or by law that is strengthened by a sense of solidarity or sharing. Ethnicity draws part of its sustenance from the concept of nationality and, not surprisingly, it uses a similar set of signifiers to define and maintain itself. One is born with one or more ethnic identities and that aspect of self may be strengthened through various statements and acts that stress one's solidarity with the whole. Those outside of the boundaries are "others", those within are folks who in some sense are "just like us". Yet the historical roots that inform members of an ethnic group that they share a distinctive identity are deeply seated in cultural traditions. Supposedly, the great American melting pot rapidly amalgamates ethnic identities, but remnants of this aspect of a person's self are quite perduring. A curious snippet may be codified in a family name, a tag end in place of birth, a shred in dialect or register (speaking style). Ethnic slurs and unequal treatment are serious reminders that elements of identity, while arbitrary and malleable, are also pervasive.

The components of a self cannot be changed overnight. In some locales, ethnic identity forms a core component of an American's self. Many such settings have members of other ethnic groups continually present and it would seem that the plurality of personalities and variety of actions would refute the stereotypes. Perhaps these refutations do occur, for the classifications of humans are constantly changing. Categorizations of group action are dialectically refashioned in day-to-day life as they confront the "token" actions of individuals that supposedly constitute a "type".

None-the-less, group stereotypes persist. The fact that Manuela, a Puerto Rican American girl in her twenties, has never had sexual relations with a male totally contradicts the white stereotype of Puerto Rican Americans as sexually unrestrained. But the group typification continues, and Manuela is, in different situations, falsely type cast and dealt with as an exception to the cultural "fact" of lasciviousness.

In The Hidden Dimension, Edward Hall expounds upon the cultural stereotypes of human interaction. He tells us, for example, that Germans "sense their own space as an extension of the ego", and that "the German's ego is extraordinarily exposed, and he will go to almost any length to preserve his 'private sphere'" (1969: 134). In contrast, he views the French "who live south and east of Paris" as typical Mediterranean sorts who "pack together more closely than do northern Europeans." They are "sensually involved with each other, (and) they have become accustomed to . . . stepped-up sensory inputs" (1969: 145). Our aim is to see if these cultural stereotypes are manifest in the range of actions employed by specific ethnic groups. If, in fact, proxemic arrangements are signifiers that help distinguish one ethnic group from another, they should vary as do community specific dialects and registers. Thus, if we can definitively show that action signifiers differ from one ethnic group to another, the groundwork will be set to talk about what these differences mean, about how the actions of a particular ethnic group relate to those of the root cultures, and how the signifiers have been adapted and given new interpretations in urban or rural settings where ethnicity is still a critical component of one's social self.

Chicago provides a perfect setting for the study since it is reknowned as one location where ethnic identity is a core defining feature of personhood. The classical studies of Burgess and Park (Park et. al. 1967; Burgess and Newcomb 1931, 1933; Park 1952), and numerous subsequent studies by sociologists from the Chicago School have dealt with ethnicity in various parts of the city. The cycles of community growth, maintenance, disintegration, and reemergence have been traced using various spatial and processual models.

The City and the press have used these studies to decide what they know about Chicago and we have used this material to select communities. As Hunter notes, the communities themselves often use fragments of the same information to help define themselves (1974). Not all communities are equally cohesive. Each group we consider is in a slightly different position in its cycle of community growth and decay, and we attempt to make note of these differences in Chapter II. But, most critically, even though boundaries shift both geographically and conceptually, the idea of an ethnic community is still a very viable concept in Chicago. In many instances, communities may be maintained as a cohesive social units as well: people live together and interact with others of similar ethnic identity; they attend the same churches and the same civic organizations; they share some political biases, class identity and they go to the same parks and beaches. Being one of the crowd who drink side-by-side in the small neighborhood bar is a core part of this social and conceptual identity. It is a signifier that says "I am a meaningful part of this group". And often, even as the community begins to disintegrate as a geographic entity, the neighborhood bars and churches remain. Both of these settings then become places where ritual exchanges take place which confirm that, "while I have moved to another part of the city, I am still committed to being part of this (conceptual) community". Even when physical communities are dissolving, ethnicity in Chicago is more than a classificatory feature of others. It is a core component of one's self, an aspect of person that often is displayed in ritual contexts of bar and church.

I

Analyzing Actions:

Proxemics in Perspective

Analyzing actions: proxemics in perspective

"The study of how man unconsciously structures microspace"(Hall 1963b: 1003). "The study of microspace as a system of bio-communication" (Hall 1963a: 442). These are the ways the anthropologist, Edward T. Hall, defines proxemics. A system of bio-communication; "unconsciously structur(ed) microspace"; hmm? Are these really the same thing? An initial aim of our research was to test the adequacy of Hall's proposed system of coding proxemic interactions; but as we proceeded, as we analyzed and asked questions, the grandiose metaphors began to sound hollow,and the basic presuppositions of proxemics came into question. This should not be surprising, for Thomas Kuhn argues the very nature of hypothesis testing brings out the anomalies (Kuhn 1962: 62-5), or reifications (Parsons 1937: 199), and the theoretical implications of a particular analytic framework. Once we began using Hall's system of coding, several contradictions began to surface. We accepted these hidden assumptions as they became apparent and continued with the research. To have changed course in mid-stream would have meant certain capsize and project failure. A retrospective look at the residual problems, though, may be of great benefit to future researchers.[1]

At times Dr. Hall's code assumes that the minimal unit act(Parsons 1937: 77) occurs in interactions between two physically distinct persons. In other cases, measures can be recorded for a single person. The kinesthetic code (body distance), for example, can only be defined for what Goffman terms a "with" (two or more persons engaged in interaction). It cannot be recorded for a single person. Voice loudness,

2

in contrast can be coded for a single physical being. So the coding procedure contains a contradiction which rests in Hall's indecisiveness as to whether action signifiers are inherently intersubjective or whether their enactment can be entirely personal and unshared.

The same problem resurfaces in a slightly different form with Dr. Hall's tendency to assume that the physical self and the social self (what Goffman calls "the actor") are, in fact, the same. The very possibility of keeping track of one person enacting several different portrayals of self is ruled out by the definition of the code. Likewise, a speech situation involving the same physical person as subject and object (as in Vygotsky's internal speech) cannot be recorded since it is presumed that the actor is always his own physical person. An inebriated man sprawled across the bar "sleeping it off", omitting occasional utterances understandable only to his alter ego is simultaneously one person (to most other actors in the context) and two selves (to himself). He cannot be recorded without violating assumptions inherent in the coding procedure. To circumvent the problem, the maps and ethnographic sketches provide a brief descriptive background for each setting, account for the presence of all actors, and discuss the uncoded effects participants have on one another.

Our supposition has been that conversation implies others, and that understanding these social selves allows the synchrony between interactants to be taken into account (even if those others are internalized). This sort of study has been conducted for small groups in a way that stresses the interactive component (Condon and Ogston 1966). The work of Labov and Fanshell (1977) further demonstrates the dynamically constituted nature of communicative events.

The measures Hall proposed apply to a disparate range of phenomena that can be analyzed on a number of different levels. He has chosen to measure some aspects of interaction

3

that are tied to the verbal portion of the speech situation (i. e., voice level, [see Trager 1964: 274-80]), while others are entirely "body behavioral" (i. e., kinesthetic or touch). At the time the research was being done, few studies of reliable quality were dedicated to the "non-verbal" aspects of interaction. Indeed, the very definition of the field as a catch-all for communicative dimensions that remain after verbal phenomena are considered, has given this form of study a residual character. As we shall argue, however, early theoreticians were pulled in directions that added as much confusion as clarity to the study of small scale interactions. Two such founding fathers, Birdwhistell and Hall, largely determined the initial direction studies of interaction, including the present one, have taken. Birdwhistell called his endeavor kinesics, the study of body movements and gestures, while Hall chose to focus on proxemics, the study of spatial relations (Hall 1968: 84). Hall and Birdwhistell share some fundamental assumptions about actions and their significance. Therefore, it is valuable to consider the relationship of research to theory for both men.

Birdwhistell, the "founder" of kinesics, created a metaphoric replica of the descriptive linguistic model to apply to the "body behavioral stream". A few elements from structural linguistics were added to strengthen suggested parallels between the structure of action and models of speech (1969: 121-140). Birdwhistell's talk of structural parallels are harmless surmising, but his implication that studies of action had confirmed the theoretical biases of his model are no more than unjustified attempts to establish authority and lend legitimacy to his speculations. The move from analogy to realized structural form is eminently apparent in his own eloquent phraseology:

These kinemes combine to form kinemorphs, which are
further analyzable into kinemorphemic classes which

4

behave like linguistic morphemes. These, analyzed, abstracted, and combined in the full body behavioral stream, prove to form complex kinemorphs which may be analogically related to words. Finally, these are combined by syntactic arrangements, still only partially understood, into extended linked behavioral organizations, the complex kinemorphic constructions, which have many of the properties of the spoken syntactic sentence (1969: 128).

His use of an active present tense convinces us that these generalizations are based on conclusive research, and the phrase "still only partially understood" leaves the impression that anything less involved than complex behavioral strings --kinemes, kinemorphs, kinemorphemic classes, and complex kinemorphs -- are a <u>fait accompli</u>. But, Birdwhistell fails to include the research that might justify the analytic units he suggests he has isolated. Without such support, we must see Birdwhistell's analogy for what it is; an attempt to legitimize for body motion a complex structural model with no analytic power.

Even the parallels suggested by this theoretical model should be treated cautiously. The clearest part of Birdwhistell's model derives from autonomous phonemics which uses minimal pairs and a process known as complementary distribution to identify analytic units. Yet Sapir, perhaps anticipating structural analogies like Birdwhistell's, was able to show that the phonological technique has a limited utility even for verbal utterances (for which it was designed) (Sapir 1949: 46-60). In the cases Sapir considers (1949: 50-51), the process of complementary distribution cannot account for the resultant phonological shapes. Even at the level of morpheme identity we encounter a situation where meaning relations must be taken into account. Thus, we should be leery of Birdwhistell's attempt to make the process of complementary distribution work for action

5

signifiers. As we learned in the course of our study, any methodology that heuristically excludes wider contexts from a consideration of units of analysis is unlikely to be able to say much about the attribution of meaning or significance.

Wider contexts of both the cultural and linguistic sort seem to be precisely what Sapir had in mind in his article. He argues that for a particular individual to comprehend two homonymous cases within any language she must not only have an understanding of the grammar but must also have a knowledge of the cultural paradigm (of which the grammar is a subset). Only in this manner will the interpretant be able to understand the sociolinguistic factors (pragmatic components) of the speech act. And by formalizing a set of rules to account for a person's knowledge of the situation or context the analyst can obtain a meaningful interpretation of an interaction.[2] On this basis, many anthropological linguists have been led to adopt a functional phonemic view that appeals to meaning and relies on both linguistic and cultural dimensions for its derivation. As Silverstein notes:

Any useful notion of meaning, I have been saying, is a product of referential meaning of the sort that contributes to the propositional values of sentences, and of the meaning contributed by another level of semiosis, the pragmatic, or cultural, or, if we follow the schema of Charles Sanders Peirce, the indexical meaning of message forms as cultural behavior. We can make precise this contribution of indexical meaning by studying empirically the ethnographic rules or use of linguistic messages (Silverstein 1973).

An approach of this sort that deals with indexicality to particular contexts is a most useful one for situating interactions. In comparison, attempts to draw distant analogies with structural linguistic paradigms hold far less promise. As many sophisticated analyses of recent years have shown (cf., Hymes 1974; Sacks, Schegloff, and Jefferson 1974; Fishman 1983; Goodwin 1981; Goodwin 1980, 1982; Blakely 1983) language and social process are one. Particular acts must, minimally, be referenced to specific situations within the modus operandi of a particular culture. Only in this fashion can the meanings of those enactments be understood. As Silverstein notes, the acts are indexical in Peirce's sense (Peirce 1932: 170-73).[3] To contend that interactive sequences are largely indexical is not to say that they are solely so; ritual sequences in particular remind us of the multi-layered signifying possibilities of acts (Turner 1969; 1970; Tambiah 1973). Nor does indexicality imply meaninglessness or lack of structure, for a number of sophisticated studies, in addition to those above, show that patterning is present and regular (i. e., Kendon 1967: 22-63; Duncan 1972: 283-292). The value of Silverstein's statement, addressed to linguists, lies in its insistence that the meaning of messages must rest at the base of empirical investigations. And meaning, he argues, is not solely of the formal propositional sort, but involves the cultural domain as well. Styles of interpersonal action clearly contribute to those cultural determinations of meaning.

In a rhetorical style similar to that of Birdwhistell, Watson has re-extended an already taut descriptive linguistic metaphor. He suggests that proxemics should seek forms analogous to those of kinesics: "I feel that the most important, and largely neglected, area of proxemic research lies in the need to isolate proxemes -- contrastive units of proxemic behavior . . ."(1972: 455). Watson goes on to suggest that for any given culture it would then be possible to identify "alloproxes of the same proxeme" (1972: 455). Like Birdwhistell's, this argument relies too heavily on the jargon of anthropological linguists who are caught up in the

7

rhetoric of phonemic and phonetic distinctions. In spite of Sapir's work, which shows the incompleteness of phonemic analysis, the very term "emic" (kineme, proxeme, etc.)has taken on a magical quality in anthropology that empowers the users of the term with privileged access to indigenous categories of the members of a culture. A closer look, however, might reveal the complex contexts of interaction that produced a certain "emic" view at the expense of many other possible views. The danger of emic metaphors thus lies in their rhetorical force, their tendency to lead the reader to believe that indigenous forms and meanings have been accurately represented. They are inappropriate to the degree that they purport to isolate contrastive and equivalent structural forms without reference to context and meaning.

In the misleading terms of the etic-emic contrast, Hall's system of coding might be called an "etic" grid. It is such a grid in the sense that it does not reflect the "emic" units of contrast of significance to a particular culture (except to Hall's own self-constructed analytic "culture"). In other respects, it is not at all comparable to the phonetic paradigm since there is no attempt to incorporate all possible units of contrast. To place any culture on this grid is not to say that its members use the units as meaningful distinguishers of action (i.e., that the units are like phonemes). Nor does it mean that the culture will select certain units from the array that includes all possible units of contrast (the phonetic ideal type). Indeed, the categories Hall has created may be totally meaningless for any particular group. They may be insignificant distinctions that are not culturally coded, or, even if the categories are recognized, they may be differentially coded by various groups (and by various sub-groups of an ethnic community). For example, the Mexican ethnic group in Chicago may have totally different

8

boundaries around what they consider "loudness" than the boundaries reflected by "loud" in Hall's code. Or, even if the boundaries around the category "loud" in Hall's code were accepted by the local Mexican community, they might argue that the label "loud" does not reflect the content and significance of that interaction style. Instead, it should be called "normal". In this hypothetical case, the category and content of "loudness" of voice are significant identity markers to members of the Mexican community that cannot be discerned using Hall's code. Gender, age, and similar factors will likewise be marked by distinctive interaction styles. Even though Hall's methods of recording interactions do not give researchers any way to capture the culturally significant contrastive units used by members of a group, they can be used to establish relative ranges of actions utilized by a particular cultural group and by sub-units of that group, depending on situation.

Indeed, Watson and Hall contend that so called "non-verbal" interactions are outside of awareness. If true, asking people about permissible behaviors or infractions becomes a meaningless technique since these actions are not consciously manipulable. If we accept Hall's contention about the unconsciousness of actions, any empirical study must imperialistically impose its own agenda since there is no option but to utilize the researcher's own rules of investigation, and her own categories. Certainly, to some degree this will always occur, but the ideal aim of any anthropological study should be to model the meaningful rules and signifying strategies of the members of a particular group. Just because action signifiers are habitual and lie largely outside of awareness, does not mean they cannot be brought to the level of consciousness. Indeed, many linguistic operations are similarly stored on the margins of our awareness, yet we do not deny that they may be brought into conscious memory. As McQuown notes

9

(personal communication), a good linguist uses eliciting procedures to force a respondent to achieve momentary focus. While analytic scenarios may require a person to bring events into relief, in many other instances people seem perfectly able to manipulate strategies of interpersonal on their own. In our culture, good examples of such conscious control include the portrayals of professional actors, the dating tactics of young teenage couples, and other newly established interpersonal relationships. Thus, there are many times when we are not consciously thinking about our communications strategies (be they verbal or non-verbal), but this does not automatically mean that they cannot be brought to consciousness and reflected upon. Claims that action signifiers are not consciously manipulable merely allow the observer to impose her own categories without exhausting the channels of research.

In our study, we have found that Hall's etic grid records many insignificant distinctions (ones that are clearly meaningless to residents of the concerned bars or churches). At the same time, the arbitrary analytic categories (i.e., vocal range of "very loud" to "soft") allows us to compare groups meaningfully across a relatively complete range of recordable patterns of action. Our use of Hall's code, then, is phenomenologically distinguishable from the "proxemes" or "kinemes" Watson and Birdwhistell discuss. We do not imply that the units of analysis are in any sense "emically" significant. They are not. And since the units reflect the categories of Hall's patterns of thinking or use, not any particular culture, these analytic units cannot be systematically combined in an hierarchical way to yield various complexes of culturally significant meaning (as can, hypothetically, kinemes and proxemes). Instead of working from minimal units to encompassing forms, we have been forced to work from relatively general situations to particular instances. The generalized context gives us a framework from which we can posit acceptable meaning scenarios. We can then identify action sequences that are either suitably tied to the status quo or systematically contradict it. Wherever possible, we have tried to identify the iconic or indexical ties that, properly or improperly, relate signifiers to signifieds. In this sense, proxemics serves as an analytic device to record potentially significant interaction configurations. It is an added level of text to be interpreted among the complex matrices of mediated meanings and intents.

Watson's approach to proxemics is one, he claims, that considers the communications act as process, yet he immediately modifies the model to suit his own ends. C. W. Morris' concept of semiosis serves as Watson's point of departure, and one of Morris' significant contributions was to view communications acts as meaningful processes (if somewhat behavioristic ones). Rather than use Morris' model as an analytic tool, Watson attempts to set up a parallel model of interaction (1972a: 20 et. seq.; 1972b: 455-57). In the process, the semantic, syntactic, and pragmatic components of Morris' model become permanently detached from one another. Rather than accentuating the interdependence of multiple meanings and structures in the communications situation (Morris 1970: 52-3), Watson loses track of these connections.

Not surprisingly, the connections between form and meaning are not left out of Watson's model simply as an oversight. His failure to deal with these inter-relationships is imposed on him by Hall's original presuppositions. (These same presuppositions limit our ability to say much about meaning.) Watson realizes that the measures he used are merely an "etic" grid (if they have an emic reality it is only to Hall and a few other investigators). Relying on his anthropological linguistic training, Watson also feels it is important to determine

11

what the significant units are within the particular culture being studied. This would allow him to say something about how the units are interrelated, about links to that which they designate, and about their relation to their interpreters (all of which Morris tells him is important). He cannot, however, identify any emic units since he claims all of the behaviors under study are unconscious. But unconscious does not mean insignificant, as Freud taught us. Here we encounter an entire arena of structures and significances. And the multitude of interpretative frameworks should not lead Watson to turn away from the mystique of the unconscious. Nonetheless, Watson becomes mystified by repressed fears of open-ended structures and covert meanings and gives up on indigenous categories and their meanings. He gives nearly as short consideration to Morris' semiotic suggestions before returning to the security of his own categorical imperatives. In this vein he tells us the task is:

. . . to attempt to construct networks and concatenations of proxemic signs. Given the lack of information concerning proxemic signs in culturally specific systems, we have no choice but to use operationally defined, phenomenally distinct, etic units in approaching proxemic behavior within a syntactic context (1972b: 457).

Even under Morris' tempering influence, Watson persists in his attempt to "concatenate" etic units into meaningful cultural forms. Morris, on the other hand, warns us that: Nothing is intrinsically a sign or a sign vehicle but becomes such only insofar as it permits something to take account of something through its mediation. Meanings are not to be located as existences at any place in the process of semiosis but are to be characterized in terms of this process as a whole (1970: 45).

Watson, thus, seems to misinterpret Morris' intent.

12

Unlike Morris who seeks semantical rules, Watson seeks definite meanings (or what Morris, above, refers to as "existences"): "What does it _mean_ when a person looks you in the eye too much or too little, or stands too close or too distant?" (1972a: 20-21). By suggesting such events have a single meaning, Watson severely distorts Morris' views on semantics and pragmatics. Morris would pose precisely the opposite question, not "what does it mean" in the singular, but "what types of things can it designate"? This view is worth quoting for it is fundamentally the same as the perspective we have adopted in our work:

The sign vehicle itself is simply one object, and its denotation of other objects resides solely in the fact that there are rules of usage which correlate the two sets of objects.

The semantical rule for an indexical sign such as pointing is simple: the sign designates at any instant what is pointed at. In general, an indexical sign designates what it directs attention to. An indexical sign does not characterize what it denotes (except to indicate roughly the space-time co-ordinates) and need not be similar to what it denotes. A characterizing sign characterizes that which it can denote. Such a sign may do this by exhibiting in itself the properties an object must have to be denoted by it, and in this case the characterizing sign is an _icon_; if this is not so, the characterizing sign may be called a symbol (1970: 24).

Watson reduces Morris' search for rules of usage to a series of one-to one correlations. Rather than building upon Sapir's related distinction between concrete and relational concepts (1949: 101-103), he seeks only direct associations.

Watson also diverges from Morris in his failure to

13

integrate what Morris terms "levels of symbolization". Instead of seeing semiosis as a total process, he segments each division of the trichotomy of signs from its complementary parts. This overlooks the probability that statements rooted in one portion of the trichotomy will operate on other levels. Morris, however, reminds us that: "Statements in pragmatics about the pragmatical dimension of specific signs are functioning predominantly in the semantical dimension" (1970: 34). This relates directly to Morris' correlary: that from a pragmatical point of reference "a linguistic structure is a system of behavior" (1970: 32). A less behaviorist perspective would also note the inverse, viz., that actions are inherently statements about meaning attributions and relations. In any case, it is unfortunate that Watson does not place more stress on the functionally interrelated meaning scenarios Morris discusses, for in proxemics one deals specifically with behaviors that are essentially pragmatic, yet they function semantically to lend particular interpretations to communications acts. The level of this functioning is primarily indexical, a point which gets lost in the jumble of etic-emic formulations that only serve to mystify parallels with formal linguistics.

Even if we consider the body behavioral repertoire as a set of indexical signifiers, each with a range of potential signifieds, problems of interpretation remain. Some are encountered when researchers encode these signifiers, others when signs are rearranged in analysis, and more when signifiers are reshaped in a written presentation for a new audience. We attempt to deal with the latter concerns with a straightforward writing style and by including enough research material to allow the reader to construct alternate interpretations. As for the selective biases of the researchers, the use of Hall's framework implies a record of rather gross-level measures. It is a code easily adapted to

14

relatively unobtrusive measurement by a systematic observer. On the other hand, the schema is notable for what it leaves out as much as for what it includes. It leads researchers to concentrate on what Duncan calls "external variable" studies (1969), and places severe limitations on information that could be considered semantically or pragmatically marked. Since we could not videotape interactions, our use of Hall's coding procedure (which recorded proxemic variables three times during a long stretch of interaction) intensified certain limits of the method. As a result, most of the structurally significant relations we were able to isolate derive from either major shifts in the interaction situation or from notable personal interaction styles of "ringleaders" around whom the action centered. A better accounting of this problem will be gained when we shift to the experimental design, the individual measures, and the recorded data. First, however, let us consider the adequacy of Hall's proposals about his proxemic paradigm.

While we use the coding procedure Hall outlined in his 1963 article, we have serious questions about a number of his findings, most of which are delineated in The Hidden Dimension (1966 [1969 edition here utilized]).[4] Hall has done anthropology a service by bringing the communicative possibilities of interaction styles to the public's attention. He has also made a contribution to the scholarly community by suggesting how much information gets communicated outside of the vocal modality. At the same time, behind his purposefully mystical title lies many a theoretical crevasse into which one might unwittingly fall. Before reviewing some of Hall's more questionable findings, we should reiterate that what Hall terms a proxemic schema is actually an etic grid. In our use of the coding system, we have tried to be systematic by applying it consistently to all of the groups considered.

Hall, however, had a different agenda in mind in

15

coining the term proxemics. The term evokes the anthropologist's supposedly unique ability to get at indigenous categories, and Hall uses that rhetoric to empower his endeavor. In spite of these claims, it is our belief that Hall, like Watson, has utilized these scales quite simply as an etic grid (see Hall 1974), even though in places he contends that the sociofugal-sociopetal distinction should be culture specific (1969: 110), and at least some aspects of his "intimate" through "public" divisions of distance should likewise vary between groups (1969: 116-125). For us, all of Hall's coding procedures are analytic tools imposed by the anthropologist in accord with his own mental categories. His labels, however, differentially imply culture consciousness. "Intimate" thus leads the reader to believe that members of the culture being investigated consider this interaction distance as one used to signify extreme familiarity. In many instances, this is not an accurate portrayal. On the other hand, people we spoke with found "sociofugal/sociopetal axis" a laughable bit of scientific jargon for such a simple idea. Who had ever heard of such a thing? Hall, then, implies that he has tapped into the semantic content of interaction processes without the use of a culturally sensitive method to ascertain meaning. In contrast, we use his grid as a tool to reveal cultural differences. We are cautious, as well, to consider content (or meaning) an essential concomitant of structure, one that cannot be imposed ad hoc on analytic categories.

Perhaps the major problem with Hall's argument in The Hidden Dimension involves his attempt to integrate studies of animal ethology with the cultural study of human groups. Undoubtedly biogenetic factors present limits to the ranges of particular behaviors, but within these given limits a great deal of cultural variation can be found. If this were the essence of Hall's argument, it would represent an

16

acceptable framework for fruitful study. Unfortunately this is not the case. Instead, he overlays polarly opposed ontological propositions. Not surprisingly, his modest attempts at reconciliation are less than successful.

Hall's first stance parades as one of total cultural relativism that rules out the possibility of a theory of human universals. Hall uses metaphors of filters and screens to play on the later writings of B. L. Whorf.[6] In this section of text, he seemingly reinforces the idea that language shapes thought and serves as a lens through which experience is perceived (cf., Whorf 1956: 252). Yet a close reading leads him to the rather different conclusion that "people from different cultures not only speak different languages but, what is possibly more important, inhabit different sensory worlds. Selective screening of sensory data admits some things while filtering out others, so that experience as it is perceived through one set of culturally patterned sensory screens is quite different from experience perceived through another" (1969: 2). Like Birdwhistell's stance, which promotes the "emicist" myth of being able to read indigenous cultures from the inside (divorced from the historicist pragmatics that lend a reality to the field situation), Hall makes the assumption that the anthropologist (more particularly he) is able to decode these sensory screens. Yet a further implication, far beyond any claims that Birdwhistell might make, is that the senses themselves are affected by culture in some mystical, unspecified, way. He rules out language as lying at the root of this perceptual differential and, unlike Whorf, gives no indication of how culture may contribute to such distinctive modes of discerning. This point is critical, for if language does not create disparate perceptual modes of functioning, and if the differential organizing principles of culture are not identified, it leads an undiscerning reader to believe the pre-perceptual modes of

17

discerning he discusses must be innate. And such a proposition, which lines up all too precisely with Hall's ethological stance, perpetuates a sort of racist reasoning that Boas and his students spent their lifetimes refuting (cf., Boas 1940).

It is most prudent to leave Hall's talk about selective screens and perceptual preconditions to psycholinguists, and subsume proxemics under a model of semiosis. If, in fact, proxemic actions and stances operate as signifiers of the iconic and indexical sort, there should be less reason to subsume them under a highly relativistic model than there was for Whorf with his interpretions of Hopi spatial and temporal semantics. The iconic and indexical elements of interaction styles should be apparent to anyone who has attempted to communicate with others in a culture whose members speak a totally unfamiliar language. If, in fact, humans inhabited different sensory worlds, like Martians and Earthlings, the possibilities of communication would be highly restricted. In actuality, we are able to "get by" by resorting to an iconic and indexical pantomime in which the ties between signifiers and signifieds are readily discernible. At the same time, however, while action sequences can be viewed as indexical to specific situations, to certain actors, to particular role relations, this is not to say they have a single necessary "meaning", that they do not function at semantic and structural as well as pragmatic levels, nor that they cannot operate as significant cultural symbols (Mead 1962: 89).

Goodenough is particularly astute in the way he integrates an action oriented approach of the sort we are advocating into a proposed theory of personal identity:

Another consideration is the occasion of an interaction. For any society there is a limited number of culturally recognized types of activity. The legitimate purposes of any activity provide the culturally recognized reasons for interactions, and they in turn define occasions. The same individuals select different identities in which to deal with one another depending on the occasion. . . . for any identity assumed by one party, there are only a limited number of matching identities available to the other party (1965: 5-6).

Goodenough goes on to note that "the parties to a social relationship do not ordinarily deal with one another in terms of only one identity-relationship at a time. . . . Some identities are relevant to all social interactions" (such as male/female, old/young, etc.) (Goodenough 1965: 7). This perspective much more adequately accounts for varied proxemic attitudes than does Hall's plea of personality differences or feeling states (cf., Hall 1969: 114). Hall utilizes personality as a catch-all to deal with anomalous findings, whereas a diverse range of identity portraying strategies all fit into the way Goodenough conceives of selves in different societies. In Goodenough's view, the "self" is not in conflict with the social order; instead, persons use their physiological forms as signifying devices to explain to others what type of fellow they may be at one particular moment and in one certain place.

As we have indicated, when read carefully, Hall's apparent relativism divests itself of its Boasian heritage and exposes itself as its own negation -- a sort of thinly concealed racism. This thread of his argument becomes more evident as he attempts to apply the findings of ethology in a direct manner to the analysis of human interaction. His "findings" here deal mainly with a series of contentions about territoriality that apply on the macro-sociological level. While it deserves clarification, it only applies indirectly to the micro-analytic framework we have borrowed from Hall. If taken seriously, however, the argument he puts forth ultimately leads to a less than totally benign

19

form of Social Darwinism or a Spencerian view of humanity.[7]

Hall begins to assemble the building blocks of his ethological edifice in Chapter II by outlining the concepts of territoriality -- flight distance, critical distance, personal and social distance -- and by delineating "contact" and "non-contact" species. Later, in Chapter X, he discusses human spatial arrangements in parallel terms:

Man, too, has a uniform way of handling distance from the fellows. With very few exceptions, flight distance and critical distance have been eliminated from human reactions. Personal and social distance, however, are obviously still present (Hall 1969: 113).[8]

Although the terminology is parallel, one might legitimately note that Hall's perspective is essentially a cultural one, for as he notes: "Proxemic behavior of this sort is culturally conditioned and entirely arbitrary" (1969: 122). Evidently, arbitrary refers to a relation of non-essentiality in the way culture has refashioned natural relationships. In this case, the acts are symbols. This statement represents one pole of the dialectic he promised to explore in his opening statements:

In light of what is known of ethology, it may be profitable in the long run if man is viewed as an organism that has elaborated and specialized his extensions to such a degree that they have taken over, and are rapidly replacing, nature. In other words, man has created a new dimension, the cultural dimension, of which proxemics is only apart. The relationship between man and the cultural dimension is one in which both man and his environment participate in molding each other (1969: 4).

In this formulation, culture, a human creation, is winning the battle in which humans and environment "participate in molding each other". Proxemics falls

20

entirely on the side of cultural order. Yet, if we look back a few sentences, we are unsure of the prioritization:

In spite of the fact that cultural systems pattern behavior in radically different ways, they are deeply rooted in biology and physiology. . . . Man has elaborated his extensions to such a degree that we are apt to forget that his humanness is rooted in his animal nature (1969: 3).

In this instance, the unique aspect of humans is rooted not in the extensions, (i. e., culture), but in animal nature, a hidden secret that culture has only served to disguise.

Inasmuch as Hall is interested in interaction, his rhetoric is notable for his generalizing not only to the level of a culture, but to the level of humanity. And as humans drop out as the realized bodies of social enactment, cultural systems (extensions) and internalized animal natures (which, for Hall, are pre-cultural) confront one another on the proxemic battlefield.

The confrontation is continued in later chapters:

Many ethologists have been reluctant to suggest that their findings apply to man, even though crowded, over-stressed animals are known to suffer from circulatory disorders, heart attacks, and lowered resistance to disease. One of the chief differences between man and animals is that man has domesticated himself by developing his extensions and then proceeded to screen his senses so that he could get more people into a smaller space. Screening helps, but the ultimate buildup can still be lethal (1969: 184).

He returns to this Robert Ardrey style of rhetoric:

. . . if men are made fearful of each other, fear resurrects the flight reaction, creating an explosive need for space. Fear, plus crowding, then produces panic (1969: 186).

In this case biology overwhelms culture, and while culture "screens" human senses, it is not able to do so effectively in crowded conditions. The image continues to be one of culture and nature combating one another on the human battlefield. "Man" and "environment" do not "mold each other" (1969: 4), they alternately determine the courses of human action. In the final instance, it is nature that prevails in this sequence of metaphors for, after all, it is not the real human, but only extensions (culture) that have hidden or filtered (screened) the reality. Fear, however, wins this battle. It pulls the flight reaction out of our human evolutionary past and brings it to bear on the present in an "explosive need for space". Here past tense has shifted to present, selective screening has been replaced by (real biological) needs, and long term processes of self-domestication, evidently a series of slow evolutionary enculturations, are superceded by violent destructive requirements of spatial pressure. "Fear + crowding = panic." His statement is formulaic. It could happen any day! These are not rational processes to be discussed, they are biological drives that can overwhelm culture.

In spite of these foreboding comments, Hall manages, through some sleight of hand, to return to his relativist point of departure. After all, fairy tales must have happy endings:

In the briefest possible sense, the message of this book is that no matter how hard man tries it is impossible for him to divest himself of his own culture, for it has penetrated to the roots of his nervous system and determines how he perceives the world. Most of culture lies hidden and is outside voluntary control, making up the warp and weft of human existence. Even when small fragments of culture are elevated to awareness they are difficult to

22

change, not only because they are so personally experienced but <u>because people cannot act or interact at all in any meaningful way except through the medium of culture</u> (1969: 188).

To our view, Hall becomes an enigma; he remains ensconced in his pseudo-scientific shell, the manipulator of mystifying metaphors. Apparently it is he who controls the key to unconscious infracultural worlds yet, on closer observation, he jumps from place to place defending contradictory contentions from which he hopes to emerge victorious. In the end there are victims but no victors, for culture and nature win in alternating moments, and the analyst, Mr. Hall, becomes entangled in the thickets beside the road. If the reader be an agile soul, she may not suffer greatly, but this is attributable to her own solid footing rather than the hand lent by Mr. Hall.

Like Birdwhistell's, Hall's position rests on a model of pattern congruity. Where the former depends on an isomorphism with the linguistic model, Hall relies on his levels of cultural relevance (1959: 44; 1969: 101) -- the infracultural, the precultural, and the microcultural (also the cultural, one would assume). As Leslie White reminds us, cultures exist <u>sui generis</u>, and current day human populations are thoroughly enculturated. Every action, as Morris reminds us, has the potential to be used and interpreted as a signifier. Pieces of human behavior cannot be sliced off of culture and called precultural or infracultural without bringing these two propositions into question. Precultural actions can only be addressed if the anthropologist resorts to the fossil record, to the analysis of indigenous cosmogenies, or to the recollections of the reincarnated. Yet the actions of living humans are not all of the same order for Hall. Some actions have cultural significance while other signifying activities (in Morris' sense) are recast into the precultural and infracultural

23

domains. There is little reason to erect these artificial boundaries among actions that all have cultural significance. Hall, however, fragments human activity into bits of behavior only some of which are cultural. When an action does not seem to fit under one rubric, Hall rejects the relevance of that analytic category, and the act is placed on another supposedly distinctive level. The residues that remain when all slots are exhausted are lumped into an amorphous designation he terms personality variation or feeling state.

Hall's pattern congruity approach comes out with greater clarity in his 1968 article (p. 91 et. seq.). In that work he takes the first draft of Hockett's design features for language, which are supposedly based on some sort of naturalness condition, and attempts to mold the pattern to fit the needs of his interactional studies. The design features selected include: duality of patterning, interchangeability, displacement, specialization, arbitrariness, productivity, and cultural transmission. Hall tells us that: "In general, the evolutionary studies of language as outlined by Hockett and the infra-cultural basis for proxemics seem to parallel each other". Hall admits that there may be points of departure, but he makes only one vaguely related comment on displacement. Indeed, displacement would present a major comparative hurdle, but had he decided to specify systematically just how other design features of proxemics "seem to parallel" those of language, he might have gotten revealed some contradictions. Duality of patterning, interchangeability, displacement, and arbitrariness, would each have proved to be major stumbling blocks.

The same sort of logic that led Birdwhistell and Watson to rely on descriptive linguistic metaphors has sent Hall in search of basic proxemic building blocks. Earlier in the same article he states:

Thus, the student of proxemics is faced with the problem of developing techniques to isolate and identify the elements of space perception. What he aims to achieve is a sense-data equivalent of the morphophonemic structure of language . . . (1968: 87).

Of course, Hall's statement is a directive to the student of proxemics, but to follow with the assertion that proxemics seems to possess all of the design features of a language leads the reader to suppose that Hall's prox_emic_ proposal incorporates the "sense-data equivalents of" the phonemic, if not the morphophonemic components of speech forms. Any such structural analogies with the linguistic paradigm are purely speculative, and none of the authors we have reviewed has discovered units that are abstractable in an "emic" manner that parallels the phonemic case. As we have argued, if there are "units" of interaction that can be identified, an appeal to meaning must be made in their delineation. For this purpose, semiotic models seem to hold far more promise than do structural linguistic analogues precisely because they consider the process of communication as a whole. This does not deny that useful, and culturally sensitive, analytic units of interaction can be isolated. Nor does it lend doubt to the proposal that hierarchical relationships may rely on pragmatic information in the semantical interpretation of utterances or sequences of action-based communication. But we see the most fruitful areas of future research as those that follow up on the connections between communicated messages and their contexts of interpretation. This is precisely because action must minimally function at an iconic or indexical level, even if it also serves other semantical functions. In its very enactment it is situationally tied, "a Representamen whose Representative character consists in its being an individual second," as Peirce would say of indexes (1932: 160). Hall readily admits that Joos' conception of the situational

25

dialect may be relevant for studies of interaction (Hall 1968: 91) and, unquestionably, Joos' view meshes well with that of Goodenough (1965), or with Goffman's notion of situational identities (1959: 107).

As it comes to be realized, however, Hall opts for a pattern congruity view rather than one based on situation specific significances. In his words: "Like all basic studies of the communicative process, proxemics, as I think of it, is more concerned with how than why, and more concerned with structure than content" (1963b: 95). Here our position and Hall's are irreconcilable. A discussion of structure without an appeal to meaning (or content, as Hall terms it) is superfluous. Berlin's and Kay's attempt to establish color categories without an appeal to meaning provides a good example of such an approach with language categories. Hall's proposals for proxemics parallel the investigative strategies of Berlin and Kay. They are even less likely to produce a fruitful result, however, since pragmatic signifiers are often used as semantic modifiers. They need not have linguistic "reference" to contribute to interpretative "sense". If Hall is serious in his suggestion that proxemics should be a purely structural endeavor, with no interest in searching for indigenous categories and meanings, his field of study should properly be designated "prox(th)etics" -- indeed, a replacement of content analysis with a search for external form. It masquerades under the "proxemic" guise as a semantic ploy to convince the reader of the culturally sensitive legitimacy of the endeavor. To justify the proxemic rubric, Hall must follow the lead of Sapir (on language), Conklin (on color categories), or Silverstein (on the relationship of language and culture); rather than overlook the matter of meaning, he must use it as an inroad to discover the basic elements of proxemic structure.

To whatever extent possible, we have attempted to use

26

Hall's coding procedures as an index of meaningful behavioral strategies. By adopting a Peircian semiotic view, we attempt to see social interaction as a series of signifying relations that can be specified by the particular situational rules of use of a given cultural group. Our work does not deny that cultural actions are constrained by biogenetic or ecological parameters. Given those absolute limits, however, we then ask the question: how do members of this culture use proxemic variables as signifiers and how are those signs interpreted by other members of the group?

In the process of research, we have found certain of Hall's distinctions to be of considerable value. For example, his discriminations among fixed, semi-fixed, and dynamic space have proved particularly valuable (Hall 1969: 103; 1968: 91). These are clearly ideal types that need not be mutually exclusive, but they function well as research tools. Most useful has been the idea of semi-fixed spaces for, while fixed space circumscribes interaction, semi-fixed objects often serve valuable signifying functions. Many of our findings about furniture use and open space parallel Hall's, and these similarities are noted in the ethnographic sketches.

Among various theorists of social interaction, Goffman approaches the problem of meaning in a serious, if not overly systematic, fashion. In contrast, Hall gives only a few snippets of cultural significance in his accounts. For example he abstracts and formalizes a set of norms for "middle-class Americans". This group, he claims, considers an "intimate" interaction distance to be within eighteen inches, "personal" space includes the next thirty inch span, and so forth (1969: 117-20). He gives little indication of how, and under what circumstances, middle-class Americans conveyed or corroborated this information. Watson's cross-cultural survey is considerably more explicit, but his method of dealing with meaning is still imprecise. Goffman, however, uses what he terms a "micro-sociological" method to look at cultural significance. The approach could equally well be considered ethnographic in that Goffman observes actions, mostly within his own culture, and imputes meanings to these behaviors on the basis of what people tell him combined with his personal knowledge about how the culture operates. While we would like to learn much more about the contexts of elicitation, Goffman often asks enough questions of a broad range of his consultants to gain a working understanding of the dynamics of interaction in cultural situations he does not know thoroughly. Goffman's "fly-on-the-wall approach (Hochschild 1983: appendix a) is always easy reading for he deals explicitly with the meanings derivable from social encounters. While he has been criticized for not adequately situating interactions in their wider contexts, an equally important issue involves his failure to include himself in the analyses. His views, always perceptive and witty, are paraded as the strategies being employed by those involved. To place a judgement on those interpretations is to question Goffman's authorial voice (Clifford 1983) and his competence as a field researcher.

What lends a consistent degree of confidence in Goffman's perceptions is his concentration on specific situations and contexts within the social milieu. In terms of Peirce's semiotics, Goffman has become skilled at outlining the meanings people impute to situated actions. He has learned to read the iconic and indexical character of interaction. Peirce, however, would want Goffman to monitor his own position as interpretant. An ethnographic presentation that dismisses elicitation contexts is a common way to substitute an oversimplified objective authority for intersubjective complexity (Clifford 1983: 121-28). While analysts of a Kantian orientation complain that Goffman has sacrificed an objective "scientific" view in order to

28

explore subjective experience, a semiotic view would note that it is precisely the intersubjectivity (in this case between Goffman and those involved in the situations he explores) that needs to be considered as a constituent element in the account (cf., Ricoeur: 1970). The interrelatedness of subjective and objective views was brought out as deserving of sociological study by Schutz (1967: 174). In his terms:

> . . . in any direct social observation carried on outside a social relationship, my interpretation of another's behavior cannot be checked against his own self-interpretation, unless of course I exchange my role as an observer for that of a participant. When I start asking questions of the person observed, I am no longer a mere observer (1967: 173-4).

Given Goffman's reliance on a similar framework of analysis, it is surprising that he does not devote more time to situating himself in the process of ethnographic production.

Our work does not attempt to reproduce Goffman's engaging and articulate style. While we deal with questions of meaning, severe methodological constraints are placed upon derivable conclusions by strict statistical controls. The sketches of settings and accompanying maps help situate the ethnographic process and lend a degree of understanding to how our information was obtained. None-the-less, a thorough study of any single setting would require months of further work. To impute unjustified interpretations of meaning to partially understood situations would bring the legitimacy of our conclusions into doubt. Therefore, we limit our conclusions to statistically obvious distinctions and discriminations. Ours is an ethnographic survey that allows us to make a few valuable comparisons among Chicago ethnic groups; it does not attempt to parade as comprehensive ethnography.

Methodological Considerations

Our study began with the analysis of bars within ethnic neighborhoods in the Chicago area. We used Hall's coding system to see if distinguishing features of ethnic activity could be documented in the non-verbal interaction styles of members of various communities. Two bars within each ethnic neighborhood were studied; the first series during the autumn of 1972, the second, a different bar within the same community in the first three months of 1973. The third sequence of research focussed on churches in the same ethnic neighborhoods, and information from these settings was gathered in the spring of 1973.

The first series of bars we analyzed provided some solid evidence that ethnic differences did exist. The second sequence of bar studies was designed to allow the researchers to obtain a more balanced range of permissible actions for each ethnic group in a certain setting. That is not to say that the contexts are identical, for the specific spatial parameters of each bar differ. Nonetheless, combining the results from two comparable settings gives a better idea of the range of acceptable action in one sort of situation. The comparison with a context that is apt to be defined quite differently, ethnic religious services, allows us to view a wider range of action signifiers that are used in cognitively disparate locations. While the measures reflect the action strategies of individual actors, their choices are shaped and monitored by social convention: if any members break the normative expectations of a particular "with", some sort of remedial work must be done to qualify

30

or rationalize the action (Goffman 1971: 108-9). In Chapter III we use non-parametric techniques of analysis to see if significant differences exist in the interaction patterns of various groups and if so, how they are used within a particular context.

We have tried to standardize our sampling procedures in order to affect each setting in the most consistent way possible. As anthropologists who have interactive effects on settings, we cannot presume to, nor desire to, reproduce the "objective" observational conditions of a study like Watson's.[9] We can only claim to have acted similarly in the various settings; the differential responses are attributable in large part to the interaction choices of those we encountered. Measurements of the proxemic patterns have been taken during the first minute after each ten minute sequence spent in a bar. The only change in this procedure occured when there was a major shift that interrupted the measurement period. In such cases, we chose to wait five minutes from the time of that change and re-take our remaining measures at ten minute intervals from that point in time. This technique allowed enough time for participants in an interaction to re-establish some sort of agreed upon spatial arrangement. It also had the effect of measuring the lulls rather than the most highly processual phases of interaction, but Hall's code is suited to precisely such an approach. It was iminently obvious to us that processes of engaging and disengaging were also highly variable among ethnic groups, but an analysis of those processes must be reserved for a future time and another technique (cf., Goodwin 1981).

Our procedure encodes situational shifts by recording the end points of the process. The method reveals the effects of the shifts that are so essential to Goffman and

31

others (cf., Whiting and Whiting Ch. XVI); at the same time, it lends an arbitrariness to the sample that psychologists consider to be advantageous. The method has obvious strengths and drawbacks. In each bar it produces a synchronic measure of the interaction patterns at three distinct and random points in time. This allows us to compare recorded patterns across situations within a single bar, between two bars, or enables us to combine measures for each bar or for groups of bars studied in order to generalize about acceptable action configurations.

We were also able to compare the interaction strategies recorded in the bars with those found in churches. We sought to obtain a maximum shift in situationally acceptable actions with these disparate settings, and yet hoped we would be able to identify some continuity in the ethnic group behaviors across the settings. As for the bars, the church measurements gave us a synchronic measure of interaction patterns; in this setting, however, we were only able to record one time sample for each church. This related to our particular methodology. After attending some services, we discovered that the patterns within the church itself were highly constrained by physical as well as normative strictures. This was fine for some measures, but for others (like sociofugal-sociopetal axis or voice level) the setting proved too restrictive. It told us some obvious things about ritual enactments in Catholic churches, but ruled out a lot of the ethnically unique patterns we could trace. On that basis, we decided to record the interactions immediately following the service -- interactions that occurred in the vestibule and the areas leading from the churches to the street.

In this context, we assumed we would be able to gain two major contrasts with the bar setting. First, the physical

32

space (semi-fixed and fixed) would have little structural effect on the patterns of interaction. On the other hand, the normative patterns that define the permissible range of acceptable actions would be more restrictively defined than was the case in the relatively "permissive" bar setting.

As in the bars, we attempted to adapt our actions to the expected patterns for the churches. In most cases, we did not try to attend the church services, but, as will be detailed in the ethnographies, we occasionally did sit in on all, or at least part, of the service. Most often, we were able to feign entry into the upcoming service while measuring the interactions of exiting parishioners. We dressed in appropriate apparel and attempted to mold our brash collegiate mannerisms to the expectations for the setting.

All churches chosen for study were either Roman Catholic or Eastern Orthodox. Again, this helped minimize the amount of variation introduced by the differences between religious orientations within ethnic groups. The major variation noted between the eastern and western Catholic churches was in the length of services. Roman Catholic mass tended to last from forty-five minutes to an hour, while Eastern Orthodox services were longer -- one continued for three and one-half hours!

We also developed strategies to standardize our actions while in the bars. We dreamed of hidden microphones and strategically placed video recorders, but settled for a few simple recording procedures. Two of us measured the behaviors simultaneously while in the bar so that we would have a cross check on the accuracy of our measures, most of which were recorded as soon as we left the bars. The maps and ethnographies were also sketched out immediately upon

33

leaving the scene and cross-checked with each other. If this could not ensure validity, it at least confirmed our common biases. In extremely active bars we found that a trip to the rest room provided a good opportunity to sketch a rough map in order to retain a maximum amount of information. In general, our slightly simplified version of Hall's code was very easy to use for recording the proxemic aspects of behavior; the two of us who noted this information seldom disagreed, and the few records that involved dispute were always minimally different (possibly a "2" versus a "20" on the distance code, a six inch variation, characterizes these disagreements).

In spite of our attempts to sit in unobtrusive locations and avoid interrupting interactions in progress, we had varied effects on the settings. We encountered diverse reactions to our presence in the various locations. In some cases we were welcomed as though we were part of the everyday clientele of a bar, or readily accepted into the neighborhood atmosphere of a church. In other cases, we threatened the very definition of community, and our initial entrances proved quite disturbing to the participants. Sometimes, these interferences were so great that we decided the resultant information was unreliable. We excluded our sample of black bars on this basis. In most bars, our ability to cope with alien situations increased throughout the research period. Toward the end of this time we felt more at ease (and undoubtedly looked more comfortable) upon entering neighborhood drinking establishments, and we began to acquire a set of strategies that would insure our acceptance within those settings. These cases are detailed in more depth in the ethnographies.

Our own characteristics also served to enhance or inhibit the reactions we encountered in different settings.

Although we dressed in a consistent manner, and one which would not in itself identify us as "graduate students", our ages (in the mid-twenties) were a feature that set us apart in an obvious way from the vast majority of the clientele encountered in the bars. These groups ranged from about thirty to sixty years of age. Age thus becomes a marker of our outsider status in most of the ethnic drinking establishments. In the churches, age proved to be a less critical distinguisher of our outsider status, since individuals of our own ages and younger were common.

Other personal attributes were symbolically coded and contributed to the emergent situation, as Goffman and his students have aptly noted in other face-to-face encounters. Our gender identities were the most obvious, and we found that the female member of the research team created the greatest stir. As noted by others (Cavan 1966: 16; Goffman 1971: 21) females may well be tabued in some types of bars, including a few of those we entered. Other characterizing identifiers such as size and appearance, which we took to be largely variable between groups, undoubtedly led to variations in others' perceptions of us. One seemingly significant factor is that we all "looked" Mediterranean or Southern European -- a conception we found to be highly inconclusive in our stereotyping of particular ethnic groups, but one which may have been applied to us as more-or-less appropriate outsiders. Finally, when asked to present identification in the bars, which did not happen often, we all showed out of state "ID's". That not only reinforced what the bar tenders already knew, that we were foreigners, it also gave them a viable means of rejecting the validity of the license without creating a great deal of disruption.

Overall, we found our greatest problems not in getting

into the bars and churches or coding interactions but, rather, in running all over the city obtaining information on the various ethnic groups, the locations of bars and churches, and the times at which these establishments were frequented. We began our search using generalities presented in the Atlas of People, Jobs, and Homes which was abstracted from the 1960 Chicago census. We supplemented this document with the University of Chicago student publication, The Avocado. Changes in the city are continuous, however, and at the time the research was conducted a more up-to-date version of the atlas had not been issued. Hence, we were often guided by sociologists, anthropologists, and friends who had a broad knowledge of the city and willingly shared their expertise with us in extensive map and automobile tours of prospective research neighborhoods.

Within the bars we decided for simplicity and uniformity to collect all of our information between the hours of 8:00 and 10:00 P. M. on week nights. We avoided Fridays, holidays, and other special occasions. As might be expected, not all ethnic groups chose to be in full force at the time of our original surveys, but a more sensitive understanding of the various ethnic neighborhoods led to better samples for our restudy. Nevertheless, we eliminated some interesting spots, such as Assyrian, and re-visited other more accessible groups, such as German, in order to flesh out the population samples and give some balance among the ethnic communities that were finally selected. Some of our original groups were dropped simply because we could not include all of the city's ethnic neighborhoods and hope for any focus or finite end to our study. Other bars were inadequately documented and required more visits to gather enough information to include them in the final sample. The ethnic communities we finally selected, while varied, each

36

have sample sizes that are roughly comparable to the other communities represented.

Before looking more closely at the coding procedures and interaction settings, we should mention Cavan's functional categorization of bars (1966). She lists four types of bars according to their purpose or use:

1) Official or manifest use: the drinking place as a spot to obtain a drink.

2) Amusement: used primarily as a setting for entertainment.

3) Private places (neighborhood bars): used in a fashion similar to one's own house or club.

4) Market place: used for the exchange of various kinds of commodities (including drugs, prostitution, homosexuality, etc.).

With this typology in mind, we set out to find ethnic bars that would all fall under the basic category of "neighborhood bar". For those establishments that obviously violated this categorization, we consumed our short beer and moved on to homier environs. On the other hand, it is important to reinforce Cavan's statements of classificatory relativity. Indeed, the neighborhood bar is a popular place precisely because, while like "one's own house" in some respects, it differs in others. Specifically, it has a manifest use, an entertainment function, and, in some instances, even a market place aspect. Each of these attributes, in differential quantity, serves to define very precisely what an ethnic bar is all about.

Cavan's functional criteria are the first step toward a semantic interpretation. While functional factors may be part of the use patterns associated with a drinking establishment, they do not exhaust how that place, and the events that transpire there, come to be defined by members of a culture. Newton (1979) uses a more sophisticated approach in her discussion of homosexual clubs. She incorporates indigenous interpretations of bars with modes of acting and presentations of self that are suited to that location. While we have not concentrated on the meanings of ethnic bars to their respective clientele, this is an area that deserves further investigation. We can say with some certainty that the way ethnic groups define and use these spaces differs considerably. Much like the church, the ethnic bar serves as a defining feature of self. It is a place where one simultaneously establishes and declares part of one's identity, and in both the bar and the church, the sharing that takes place therein expresses the solidarity of the group. Of course, there are rituals of exclusion as well. These demarcate differences among insiders and define the boundaries outside of which one encounters only outsiders.

We do not focus on the ritual sequences, but rather on the settings in terms of which segregation and unity are differentially coded. When rules are broken, reparative actions or remedial interchanges take place to draw the actions back into line or to make up for some faux pas (Goffman 1971: 108). In other cases, we talk of paralinguistic or proxemic markers in a way analogous to the discussion of linguistic markers -- to describe various deictic or indexical patterns. We also pay close attention to anomalies, and to various unusual interactional configurations that do not seem to fit the cultural pattern. Hall would describe these exceptions to the rule as being the influence of personal emotional state, that is, as modes of acting that fall outside of the cultural pattern. In contrast, we consider situational factors that may contribute to such forms of action. The actions are thus appropriated within the broad range of cultural configurations whose variant modes of expression and

38

interpretation depend upon their contexts of use. There are many examples, but the anomalous kinesthetic score in the Greek church, and the unusual configuration that concentrates on the old man in Italian Bar #16 indicate what can be learned from these instances. We use contextual appropriateness as a method of deciphering and re-encoding cultural significance. In so doing, we hope to contribute to a theory that allows varied ranges of personal action to fit comfortably within phenomenologically diverse modes of cultural expression. This does not deny that certain forms of action are "unthinkable", only that when they happen, there are culturally appropriate ways of restructuring events and occurrences to account for them.

Table I presents Hall's code (1963) along with the modified version that proved to be best adapted to our needs. No changes were required to make the "sociofugal-sociopetal" and "kinesthetic" scales useful, and to the postural-sex identifiers we added a means of coding males and females seated on bar stools. Most highly altered is the "touching" code. We simplified it to eliminate the highly subjective interpretative distinctions from "caressing and holding" through "extended or prolonged holding". The "voice loudness" and "vision" codes were simplified, not to imply that other boundaries are less appropriate but, rather, to adapt them to our research design. A simple numeric label is used to refer to the categories within each domain measured. This should help eliminate the impression that the boundaries between categories are meaningful to local participants (see discussion in Chapter I). These scales of measurement comprise the grid in terms of which group comparisons are made throughout the remainder of the text. They should be readily comparable to the distinctions used by Watson in his study.

In the ethnographic sketches that follow, "R" indicates the researchers' location.

TABLE I

Postural-Sex Identifiers:

	our code	Hall's code
man prone	1	1
woman prone	2	2
man sitting	3	3
woman sitting	4	4
man sitting at stool	5	-
woman sitting at stool	6	-
man standing	7	5
woman standing	8	6

Sociofugal-Sociopetal axis:

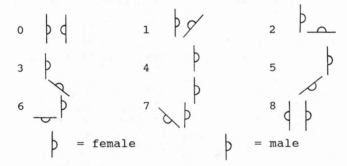

Kinesthetic factors:

     1 - within body contact distance
   10 - just outside body contact distance
    2 - easy touching distance - forearm extended
   20 - outside forearm distance ("elbow room")
    3 - within touching distance - arm fully extended
   30 - outside this distance
    4 - within reaching distance - two arm's length
   40 - just outside reaching distance
   50 - no potential - eight feet or more

TABLE I - continued

Touching:

	our code	Hall's code
caressing and holding	0	0
feeling or caressing	0	1
extended or prolonged holding	0	2
holding	1	3
spot touching	2	4
accidental touching	3	5
no contact whatever	4	6

Vision:

	Hall's code
foveal (sharp - direct eye contact)	-- 1
macular (clear - concentrated on the person)	-- 2
peripheral	-- 3
no visual contact	-- 4

(Hall codes "no visual contact" as an "8")

Voice loudness:

	our code	Hall's code
very loud		6
	4	
loud		5
	3	
normal+		4
normal		3
	2	
soft		2
	1	
very soft		1
silent	0	0

42

II

Ethnographic Sketches

Mexican: Bar #1--El Rebozo

The first Mexican bar in our sample is located on
Armitage between Damen and Western. The bar is called El
Rebozo. Armitage seems to serve as the dividing line
between a Mexican neighborhood and a sizeable Polish
neighborhood. A few blocks north of Armitage can be found
one of the Polish bars as well as the Polish church sampled
in the second part of the study. On the south side of
Armitage are several establishments bearing Spanish names,
including El Rebozo.

Following our usual procedure, we requested three
glasses of beer. The bartender painstakingly enumerated, in
heavily accented English, the brands of beer stocked. We
specified our preference and were served without being asked
for identification. El Rebozo was not as well appointed as
the other bars we visited. There was a good deal of
barroom "ad art", but it was of the old neon sign type
promoting a particular brand of beer. A black and white
television and a jukebox were in operation simultaneously,
although they were no more than fifteen feet apart. On the
cash register was a "Madonna" holy card. There were also
some dollar bills tacked to the wall behind the cash
register.

Several tables were along the wall opposite the bar.
At one of them four men were seated (see map), engaged in a
game of dominoes. Eye contact among the players was

44

restricted to their dominoes, with some peripheral eye contact across the table. After each hand there was cheerful conversation between the players gathered around the game table. They shook hands, laughed, and talked loudly.

At the left corner of the bar was a separate triad of males. They were engaged in quiet conversation. One of the members of this group left the bar shortly after our arrival and returned within a few minutes. He then took a seat near the domino table and kibitzed the game.

At one point the senior member of the domino game asked the female member of our research team if she spoke Spanish. She replied, in her hesitating Caribbean dialect, that she did not, whereupon the man turned back to his companions and said, "What are they doing here if they don't speak Spanish?" (As might be guessed, this entire dialogue took place in Spanish.) The gentleman who posed the question was the dominant figure in the bar. He controlled the whole tone of the interaction. It seems that he had seated himself in a strategic position since, he was facing the door and could see all who entered the bar.

The bartender did little with the exception of getting beer for the customers. He did, however, talk to the investigators for a few minutes. On one occasion a customer simply stepped behind the bar to get himself another beer.

After the domino game had ended the men got up from the table, remaining in the same interaction dyads, and continued their conversations, some sitting at the bar and the others standing. There was one man who was out of the mainstream of the action. He sat at the bar with his drink in hand, occasionally looking up at the television.

Our overall impression was that the clientele was not disturbed by our presence in spite of the remark mentioned earlier. They seemed to be curious. When we left most of them said 'goodby' or made friendly gestures. The bartender asked us to come back sometime. Once outside we looked back and noticed that several of the men had come to the window to watch us leave.

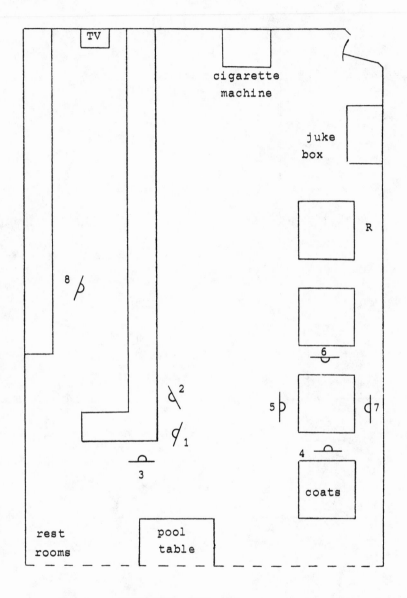

MEXICAN BAR #1   time 1

47

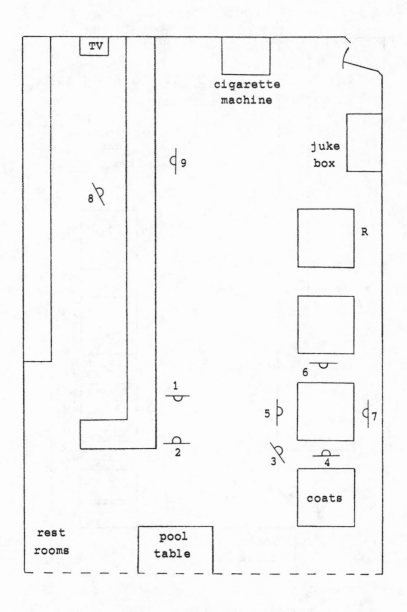

MEXICAN BAR #1   time 2

48

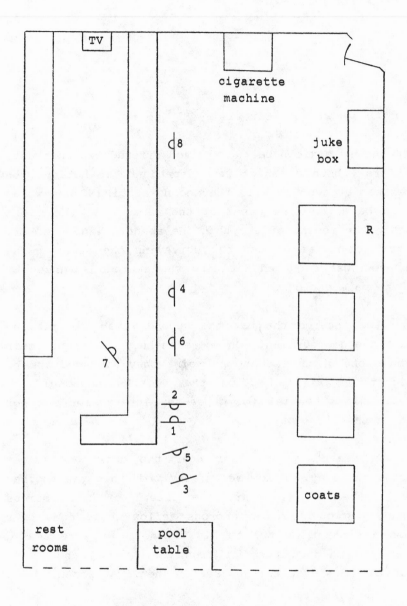

MEXICAN BAR #1   time 3

49

Mexican: Bar #11 -- El Capitan

The second Mexican bar we visited offered two contrasts to the first, both of which were dependent, we believe, on the presence of two women in the second setting. One woman seemed to be either the owner or the manager of the bar. Other than the moment or two that she spent behind the bar, the first woman sat at the bar surveying the scene. The second woman was occupied fielding the amorous advances of one of the male patrons.

When we entered the bar the second woman was playing pool with the amorous man. On occasion they would put their arms about one another. At one point they embraced and he affectionately kissed her on the neck. As could be inferred, this potential for cross-sex interaction was not present in the first bar.

A man seated at the bar near the door was asleep throughout our stay. A few seats away from this man another man was seated at the bar, the friend of the amorous gentleman. Frequently the amorous fellow would come over and pass a comment or two to his friend. We were seated four bar stools down the bar from the friend, and a few seats further down the bar was seated the first woman.

At the back of the bar there were three men seated at a table. These men talked among themselves throughout our stay. Prior to the time two measurement, two of the men

50

moved closer, further isolating their conversation. There was some touching within this group. None of this conversation was audible to the investigators.

As might be expected, there was a great deal of interaction between the second woman and the amorous gentleman. Except for the first few minutes following the pool game, when the gentleman talked with his friend, he and his lady friend sat very close to each other -- talking, touching, and sometimes giggling. The friend was not included in most of the interaction. All of the conversation, including that between the gentleman and his friend, was in hushed tones. This offered the other contrast to the first Mexican bar visited. The difference in the overall noise level between the table game setting of the first bar and the courting ritual of the second bar was striking.

In regard to the physical setting, the differences between the two bars were negligible. There was a pool table, a jukebox, and a television set which was not in use. The jukebox was played a couple of times. As in the first Mexican bar the bartender was male. However, in this case, the bartender did not speak English. We ordered beer, and after the bartender roamed around looking at bottles, we caught his attention and ordered in Spanish. Above the liquor cabinet were several bills -- some ones and a five dollar note. There was also a five hundred peso note.

A bit later, prior to our taking the measurements at time three, three men entered the bar. One of them stood and talked to the first woman. Another talked with the bartender briefly, while the other went behind the bar in the direction of the bartender. When the third man began talking with the bartender the second stepped back from the

51

bar, while the third moved very close to the bartender and talked with him. Both were standing.

With the exception of waiting on customers, the bartender stood behind the bar near the corner where the sleeping man sat, and appeared to be either reading or writing. The first woman sat at the bar; she did, however, serve the men at the table once and passed a few words with them.

Goffman (1971, 256) notes the importance of entrances and their function for orientation. This was seen immediately following the entrance of the three men. Prior to their entrance, the amorous man had gone into the restroom, and when he returned the three men were present. This man made a slow and almost dramatic entrance in which he seemed to be "looking over" the new arrivals (reorienting his performance). He took his seat and continued with his woman friend, though in a slightly restrained manner.

All the conversation was in Spanish. Four marked cases occurred during this visit. These are interactive strategies that were not typical for the setting. That does not mean the actions were tabu, but that they were being used as special signifiers to mark specific behavioral messages that were being communicated within the larger interaction framework of the bar. Two of the marked cases were recorded on the kinesthetic (distance) code. The first of the two observed on kinesthetic occurred in an interaction between the two women in the bar. At this time the amorous gentleman was playing pool with the second woman (person #2 on the map), and she briefly conversed with the first woman. This was coded as a "5" (no potential for contact). The second marked case on the kinesthetic code occurred at the time two between two men seated at the bar

-- the amorous man and his friend. The second woman was
seated between the two men.

The two marked cases recorded on the touch code
involved the same pair of interactants in both cases -- the
amorous gentleman and the second woman. In both cases the
interactants were engaged in prolonged holding or touching
of each other. Both cases were coded as "O's".

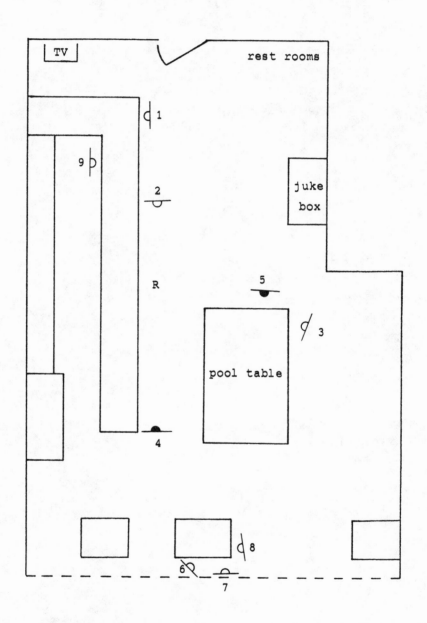

TV

rest rooms

juke box

1

9

2

R

5

3

pool table

4

8

6

7

MEXICAN   BAR   #11   time 1

54

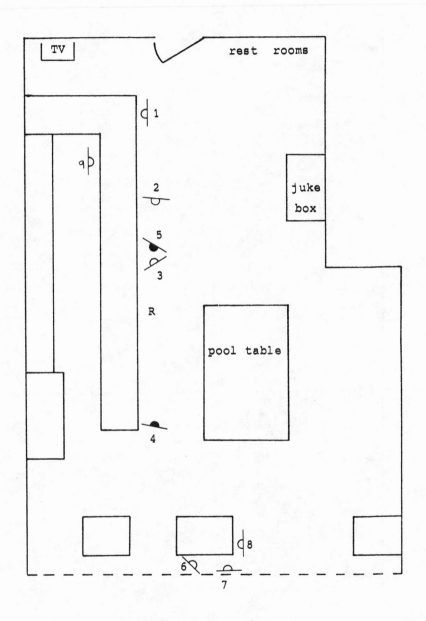

MEXICAN BAR #11   time 2

55

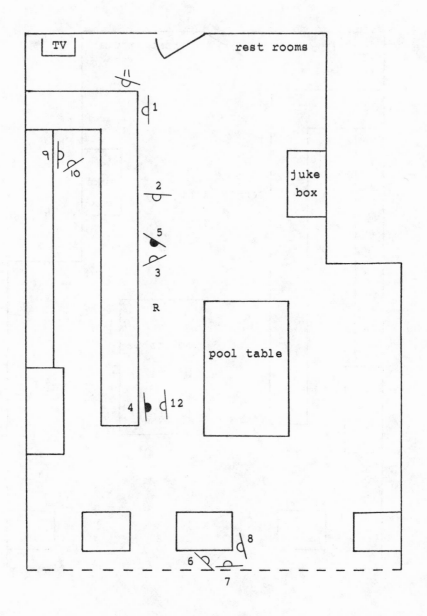

MEXICAN BAR #11   time 3

56

Mexican: Church #21 -- St. Diego

Our Mexican church, located on the city's southwest side, is in a transitional neighborhood; the older residents being eastern Europeans. Not all of the parishioners were Mexican and conversation was for the most part in English. Only those people who were obviously of Mexican extraction were coded in interactions. These interactions were sustained for a longer duration than those of our other groups. The extended conversation period may have been due to the nice weather or to different norms within the group. In any event, the length can only be noted as Hall's measures do not allow for the measurement of this variable across interactions. Quantification of interaction time has not been made, but it would seem to be a worthwhile variable for any future researchers attempting to improve upon Hall's code. There were no marked cases in our observations, and the data revealed no inconsistencies with our earlier Mexican bars.

The church was of older red brick construction with a sizeable vestibule which was not utilized for conversation. The people preferred to go outside to the front of the church and group on the fifteen foot wide sidewalk. The church is located on a busy residential street with private residences on all sides but only one block from a main thoroughfare with small shops.

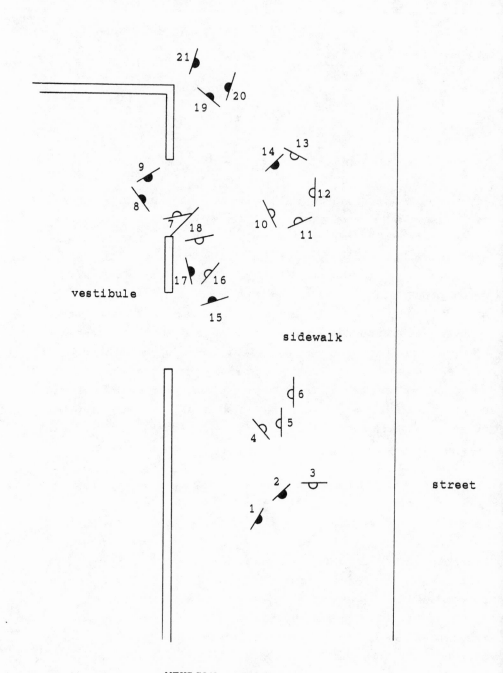

vestibule

sidewalk

street

MEXICAN   CHURCH

58

Polish: Bar #2 -- Stanley's

The first bar visited in the study was also the last bar visited. This may sound confusing, so an explanation is in order. The first time Stanley's was visited, we met with some difficulty. Upon our entry, the conversation in the bar ceased but picked up within a few moments. After some searching we located the bartender who was standing at one end of the bar with several customers. He asked if he could help us. We ordered three glasses of beer. He then asked for our identifications. After a cursory glance at our driver's licenses he said that the identifications were unacceptable--so we left. This was on November 3rd.

On April 25th of the next year we decided to try again. We entered the bar and looked for seats. A man at the corner of the bar hailed us and said that there was room at the section of the bar where he was seated. He immediately began talking with one of the investigators. Thereupon the bartender came over and asked what we would like. We ordered beer, and again he asked to see our identifications. After a cursory glance at our driver's licenses, he again asked us for our order.

It seems that there were several factors working in our favor on this second occasion; factors that were not present on the first visit. To begin with, there was no reaction, or at least minimal reaction, on the part of the clientele with the exception of the patron who invited us to sit with

59

him. The second factor was that the customer seemed to accept us immediately. Third, since the November encounter when we had been refused service at this bar, we had visited twenty or more bars and were now more poised and able to adapt quickly to a variety of barroom situations.

There was a color television behind the bar at the far end. A jukebox and an electric bowling machine were also available for the patrons. Fourteen people were lined up at the bar -- twelve along one side and two at the short side. All of the interactants were in dyads and triads, which made for regimented distance patterns within interacting groups. Outwardly this distance would seem to contradict the kinesthetic patterns seen in Polish bar #12, but the variations can be accounted for by the structural necessities of the particular setting. That is, in this bar the distance between interactants was structured by the crowded seating arrangements at the bar (See map). Yet if one looks at the touch scores in both bars, no notable differences are discernible. The sociofugal and sociopetal scores also reflect the physical structure of the bars. This structuring effect will be dealt with in the data analysis. This fits well within Goffman's comments on the structuring of "withs". Certain situations will structure to some extent particular aspects of interaction patterns (Goffman: 1971:202-203).

One thing that stands out in this bar is one case of extended foveal eye contact recorded on the visual scale. No such score was recorded in the second Polish bar. This eye contact occurred in a cross-sex interaction. The woman was coded as a "1" on visual (Foveal eye contact) at times "2" and "3" with the same man. From what we could gather in overhearing the conversation, we assumed that this man was not the womans' husband but that the man seated between them

60

was her husband.

It is possible that extended foveal eye contact in such a setting is a cross-sex identifier within the Polish group. Although our data on this point is too shallow to support such a notion, it may be worthy of further investigation. If such an identifier of cross-gender interactions exists, it might be culturally specific, though same-sex foveal contact is quite common among the Greeks, Italians, and Mexicans studied.

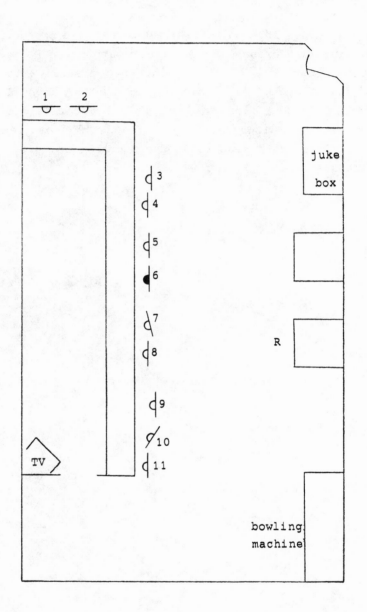

POLISH   BAR   #2   time 1

62

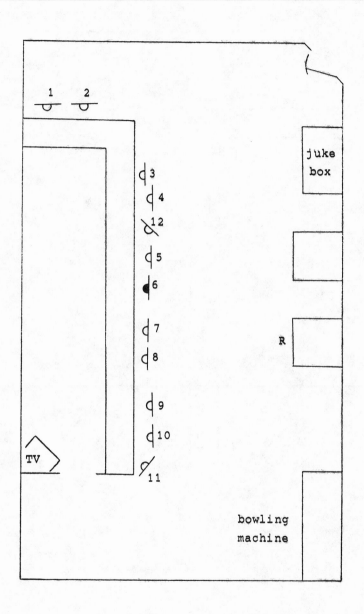

POLISH   BAR   #2   time   2

63

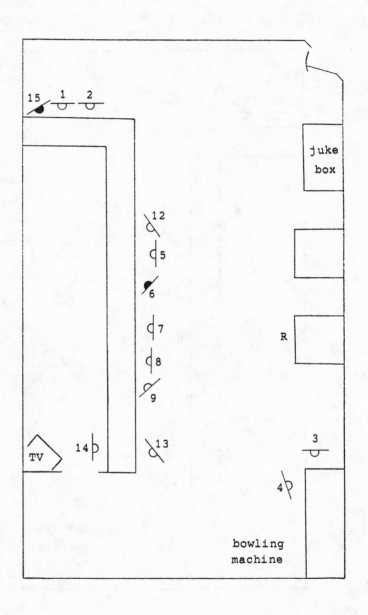

POLISH   BAR   #2   time 3

64

Polish: Bar #12 -- Gonskas

Gonska's, the second Polish bar in the study, is located on 21st Street near Oakley. The neighborhood seems to be rather mixed. Along 22nd Street are many establishments bearing Spanish names. The second Mexican bar in the sample is within a few blocks of Gonska's.

Physically this bar was much like the other bars in the study. As was the case in the first Polish bar, the tables here were not used. All of the patrons sat at the bar. There was a television behind the bar, a jukebox, and a pool table. Hats and coats were strewn on top of the pool table. In the first Polish bar the pool table was used for playing pool, while the tables were piled high with hats and coats. Also, there was an electric penny arcade type shooting gallery machine, and bowling trophies were on display above the liquor cabinet. Occasionally the mynah bird would whistle or say "Hello". As in the first Polish bar, there was an electric bowling game.

It was noted previously that the kinesthetic scores in both bars differed, but, as one can see by looking at the maps, this reflects the spatial relations structured by the seating arrangements at the bar. In spite of the greater distances between interactants in this setting, the touch scores on the lower level of the scale (that is spot touching and holding) do not differ notably.

65

One marked case was observed in this bar. This occurred on the touch code at time three. The interactants in this case were husband and wife, which fits in with most of the cases where a touch score was markedly low for that particular ethnic group. Touch as a marked case will be discussed at greater length in the data analysis.

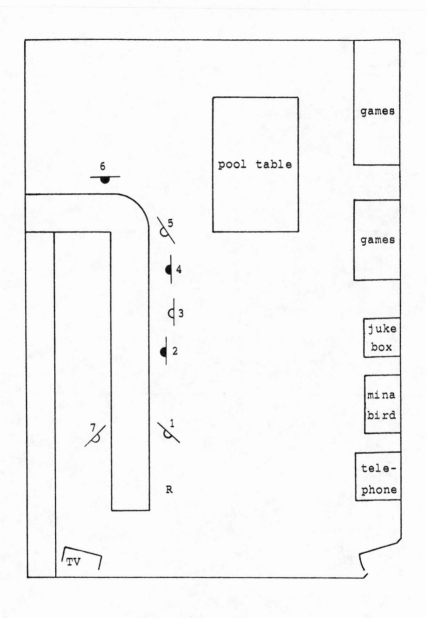

POLISH BAR #12   time 1

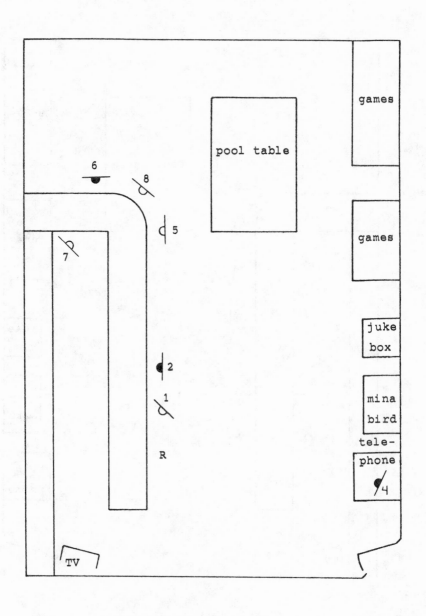

POLISH   BAR   #12   time 2

68

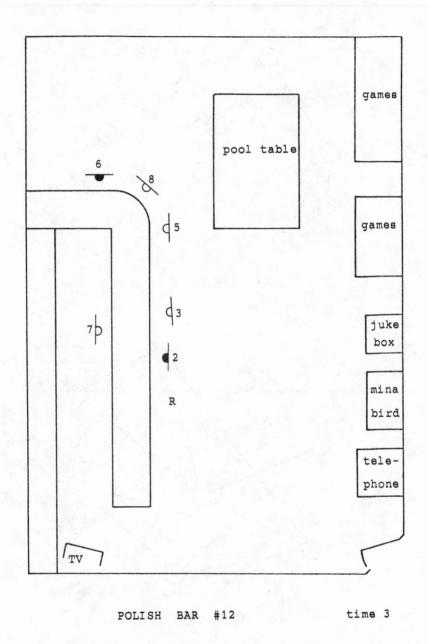

POLISH BAR #12   time 3

A Network Comparison of Interaction in Polish Bars

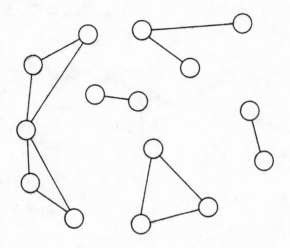

Polish Bar #2

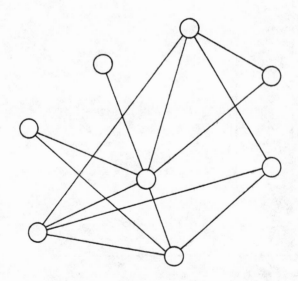

Polish Bar #12

Polish: Church #22--St. Nicholaus

    Our Polish church was in the same neighborhood as
Stanley's, the Polish bar. It was located on a quiet street
of older single family dwellings.   There are two main
buildings: 1) a social hall, west of the church where
people went for refreshments after the service, and 2) the
church itself.   St. Nicolaus's is a fairly large stone
church with wide steps and rails leading up to the
vestibule. Inside the vestibules on the east side was a set
of stairs leading down beneath the church to the women's
bathroom and classrooms.   As with the German church, we
coded the interactions directly following the 9 a.m.
service.   The service was conducted in Polish.   Unlike the
German neighborhood, the Poles are still a socially cohesive
ethnic group in this particular area.   The railings running
down the stairs serve to structure the interaction space to
an extent as they did with the Greek church (c.f., the old
woman-young girl touching dyad in both instances).   In the
rest of this relatively unstructured setting, there are more
face-to-face interactions than in our Polish bars.   As can
be seen on the map, most interactions took place in three
distinct spatial clusters -- in the church, on the steps,
and on the wide sidewalk directly in front of the church.
The longest lasting sets were those on the sidewalk and in
the vestibule.   The vestibule was fairly wide and large with
pillars which separated the interaction sets.   Only women
were observed interacting in the vestibule, which may have
been affected by the close proximity of the ladies washroom.
Males were better represented outside the church.

71

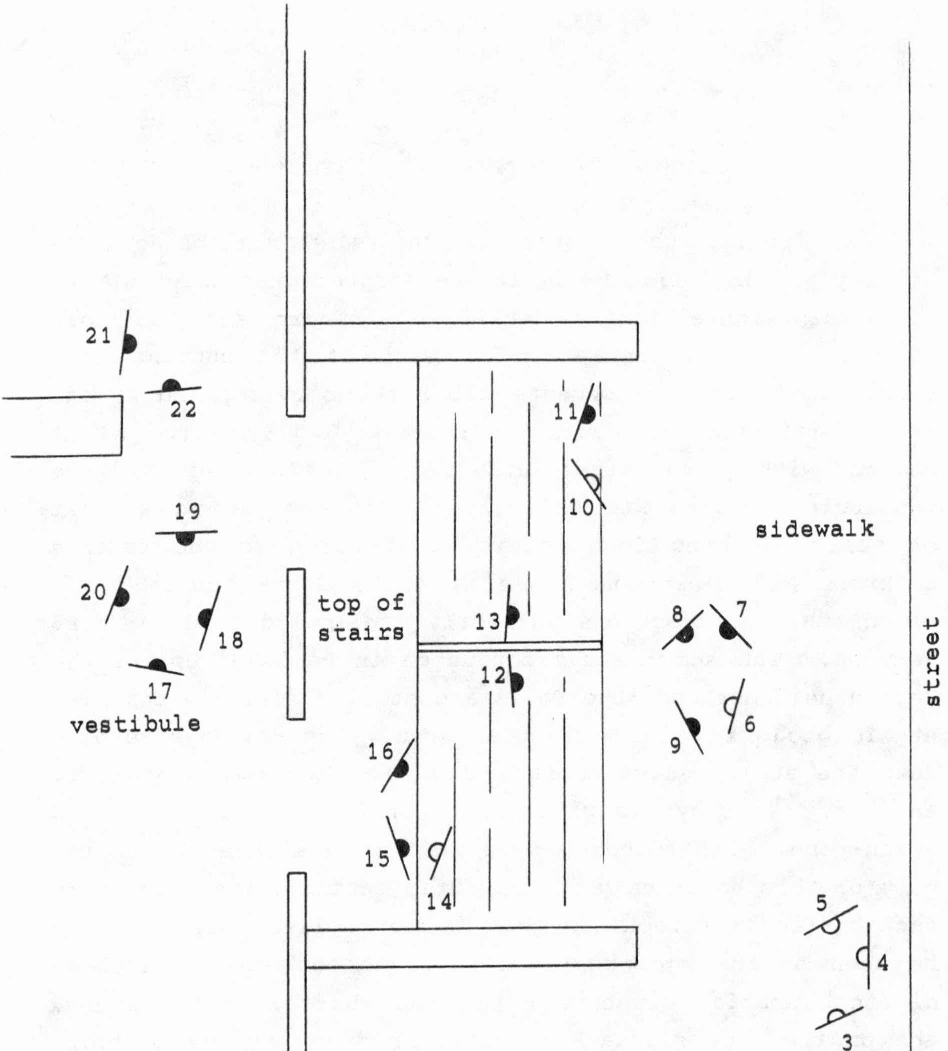

21

22

19

20 18

17

vestibule

top of
stairs

sidewalk

11

10

13

12

16

15

14

8 7

9 6

5

4

3

2 1

street

POLISH CHURCH

72

German: Bar #4--Das Hofbrau Haus

Das Hofbrau Haus is located on Lincoln, a mile or so from the Rathskeller.   Six people were present when we arrived.   Two men, a woman, and a young boy were seated near the corner of the bar (see map).   Another man was seated at the same side of the bar, but toward the other end.   The bartender was male.   He and a single male customer watched the color television for most of our stay.

The bar is rectangular with the liquor stock in the center.   The television was attached to the rear wall, providing an unobstructed view from every seat.

Most of the interactions took place within the group of four seated near the corner of the bar away from the television.   All of the conversation was in German.

There were two cases where the measurements taken were atypical for the German sample as a whole.   The first of these occurred at time one and involved a same sex dyad on the sociofugal-sociopetal axis measurement.   Person number 2 was watching television while carrying on a conversation with person number 3 (see map).   Their shoulder axis was recorded as a "5", and the conversation was over number 2's shoulder.   Hall notes (1963:1009) that "Position 6 is used as a means of disengaging oneself.   It is not quite, but almost as, sociofugal as 8".   It seems that position 5 could also be regarded as a means of disengaging oneself, and in

73

this case it is apparent that person number 2 has divided his attention between the television and his conversation with person number 3.

Hall, in the same article (1963:1009), says that position 4 "is one in which two people are normally watching and/or discussing something outside themselves, such as an athletic event---". In this case position 5 may be regarded as a transitional phase between engagement in an interaction (position 4) and disengagement (position 6).

The second interaction deserving note involved a case of cross-sex touching occurring at time two between individuals of different age. The parties to this interaction were a woman and her young son (about nine years old). The observation was recorded as "1" (holding) on the touch scale.

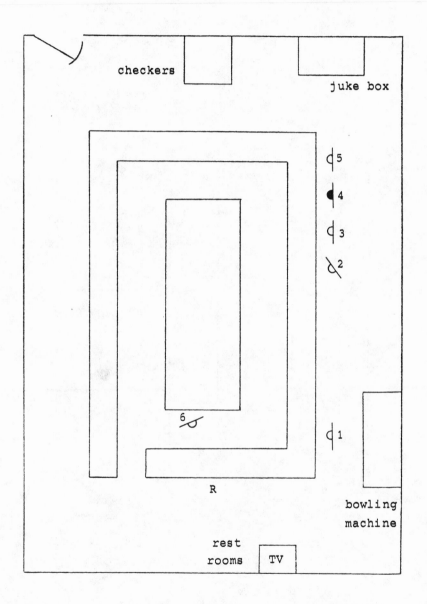

checkers

juke box

5

4

3

2

1

6

R

bowling
machine

rest
rooms   TV

GERMAN   BAR   #4   time 1

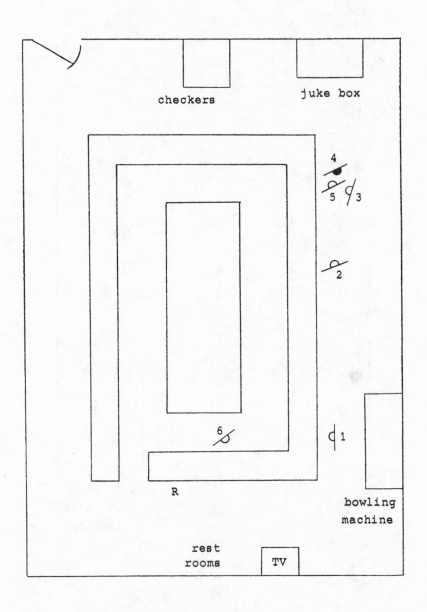

checkers   juke box

R

                              bowling
                              machine

rest
rooms   TV

GERMAN   BAR   #4   time 3

76

German: Bar #5--The Rathskeller

The Rathskeller is located on Lincoln near Montrose.
The interior was decorated much like a Bavarian Chalet with
wood paneling and rough hewn beams traversing the room. At
the time of our arrival there were thirteen people present
including the bartender. All of the people in the bar spoke
German.

When we entered, the clientele seemed more disturbed
than in the Mexican bar. The overall noise level dropped
abruptly but picked up within a few minutes. The lighting
in the Rathskeller was brighter than in the Mexican bar and
nearly as bright as the Italian bar. There was no
television.

Throughout our stay there was quite a bit of moving
about. Shortly after we arrived the man at the right end of
the bar exited. Soon after his departure a dyad at the left
end of the bar broke up, with one man taking a seat at a
table with the bartender who had come out from behind the
bar.

A man and a woman were seated at the middle of the bar
at time one. At time two the man departed and another man
from the dyad at the left end of the bar moved down and was
seated next to the woman. Formerly there had been two bar
stools separating the interactants, but by time three each
had moved over one stool. The man put his arm around the

woman's waist and was moving his hand down her hips when she removed his hand. This proved to be a marked case of touching in this bar. It is the only instance where any touching more prolonged than spot or accidental occurred, and the woman's response shows her disapproval of the action in this setting. Most of the touching in our German sample was spot and accidental as defined previously.

Also there was an odd shoulder axis configuration recorded on the sociofugal-sociopetal measure at time two. This case involved a male-female interaction. The shoulder axis was recorded as a "5" (see section on Sociofugal-Sociopetal coding definition). The man was seated, the woman was standing, and the conversation was carried on over the man's shoulder with only peripheral eye contact noted.

The group of men at the right corner of the bar got up at time three, came over to the table and said goodby to the bartender and others seated there. They then exchanged handshakes before leaving the bar.

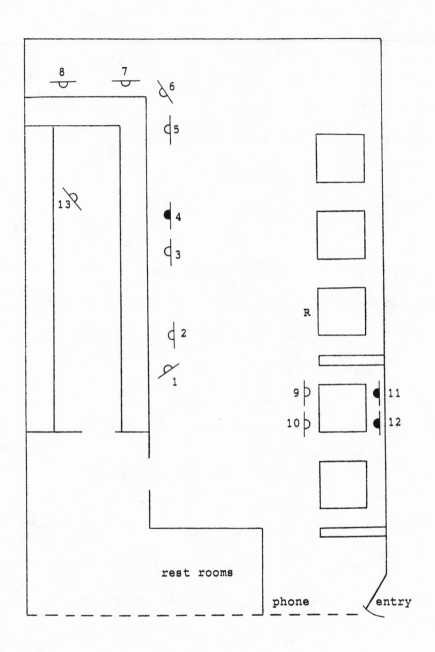

GERMAN   BAR   #5   time 1

79

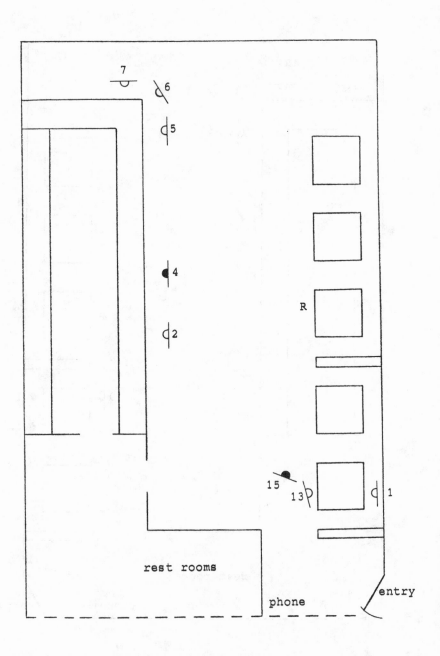

7

6

5

4

2

R

15
13
1

rest rooms

phone

entry

GERMAN   BAR   #5   time 2

80

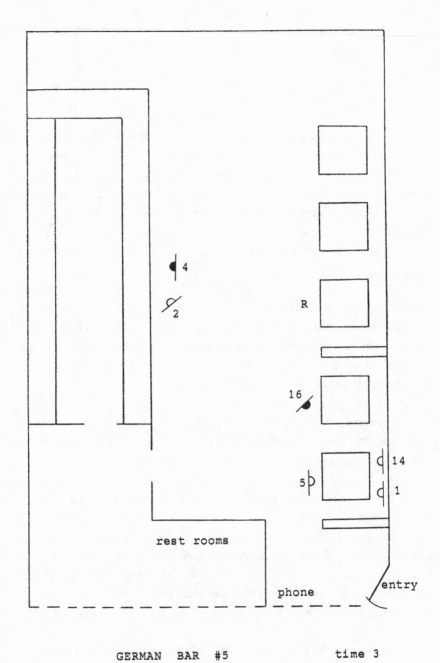

R

rest rooms

phone

entry

GERMAN   BAR   #5   time 3

81

German: Bar #15--Straussberger

The third bar in the German sample can also be found on
Lincoln near the others. This bar, the Straussberger, is
well lit and more nicely decorated than the Rathskeller but
generally in the same decor. Ornate beer steins and
glassware were on display in the bar area.

The maître d' greeted us cordially and seated us at the
bar. There were eight people at the bar, not including the
bartender, a gentleman in his sixties. The maître d' stayed
at the right corner of the bar where most of the action was
taking place, speaking with a group of four customers who
all seemed to be good friends.

Unlike other bars visited, there was neither a
television nor a jukebox. Behind the bar section was a
large dining room.

As noted above most of the action took place within a
group at the right corner of the bar. This group told jokes
of the "Polish" variety. The conversation was partly in
English and partly in German. At one point during the joke
telling the maître d' looked up at the investigators and
said that it was allright for the gentleman who was telling
the "Polish" jokes to do so because he, the joke teller, was
Polish.

This is interesting in light of Hall's comments on
Germans' feelings regarding visual intrusion. He comments:

"For the German, there is no such thing as being inside the room without being inside the zone of intrusion, particularly if one looks at the other party, no matter how far away." (1969:134)

In this instance, our presence in the room and our occasional glances, in violation of their private sphere, moved the maître d' to take "reparative action" to excuse the behavior of the joke teller and his "with".

The bartender did not participate in the conversations at either end of the bar. Occasionally he would laugh at a joke or laconically reply to a question.

There were three females in the bar, one of whom was the barmaid. Again, as in the first German bar, there was a young boy (12 years old) present.

Two observations proved to be notable cases. One of them, on the visual scale, involved the man who was telling the "Polish" jokes. This man was the center of attention in the group at the corner of the bar. At time three he maintained foveal eye contact with the maître d'.

The other unusual case was noted on the sociofugal-sociopetal scale. This was recorded as a "6". The maître d' was talking to a woman, and she was replying over her shoulder. Again this sociofugal configuration involved a cross-sex interaction.

Hall's comments (1969:136-138) with regard to Germans' use of fixed and semi-fixed space corresponds with our observations in all three German bars visited. In all three settings the patrons did little in the way of moving the furniture about. This was not the case in many of the other

83

bars, such as the Italian and Mexican bars, where furniture was often repositioned.

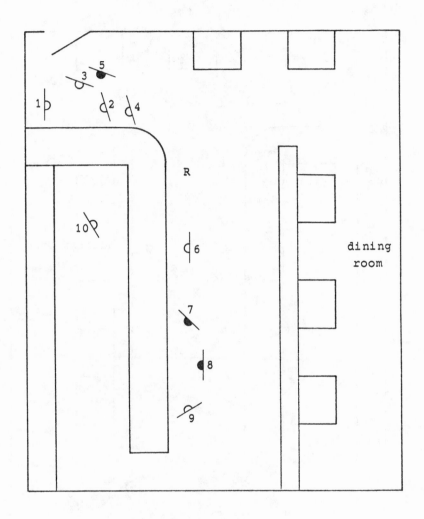

GERMAN   BAR   #15   time 1

85

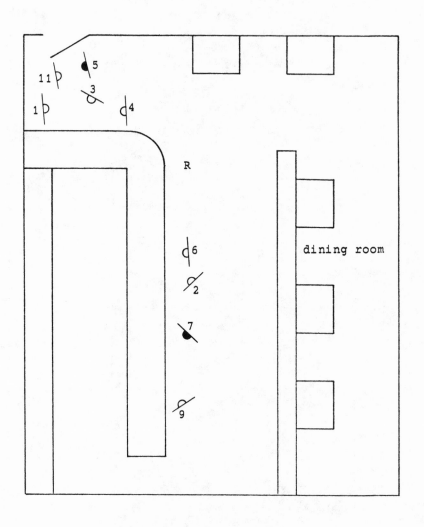

R

dining room

GERMAN   BAR   #15   time 2

86

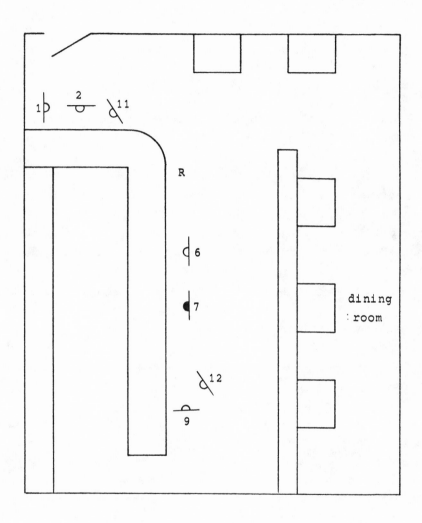

GERMAN   BAR   #15   time 3

87

German: Church #25--St. Peter's

St. Peter's is a tremendous stone church located at the intersection of three main boulevards on the city's near northside.   Possibly because of the busy streets below, the builders constructed a huge circular terrace with a stone balustrade ten feet above street level.   As can be seen on the map, there are two sets of stairs leading down to the sidewalk from the terrace, and the church's three main entrances are all approached directly from the terrace.

There was only one service given in German, and it was fairly early in the morning at 9 a.m.   The neighborhood is in transition with many of the parishioners not of German heritage.   We sampled immediately after the German language service in an attempt to not confound our sample with non-Germans.

Despite the large terrace and the fact that it was a most pleasant day, the people did not strike up conversations after the service.   They seemed rather to be fleeing the surrounds.   In any event we coded only those interactions where people paused long enough to talk to one another upon leaving the church.   The largest interaction cluster was among two priests and some parishioners in the main vestibule.   This was one of the few "withs" that stayed together for any length of time to actually carry on a conversation.   The only observed atypical case was on voice level where a woman was listening to a priest but not speaking herself. Her passive actions were clearly acceptable for the specific interaction in which she was engaged. The Germans, along with the Irish, appear to touch the least and utilize the widest range of interaction space. (The kinesthetic measures range from "10's" to "40's".)

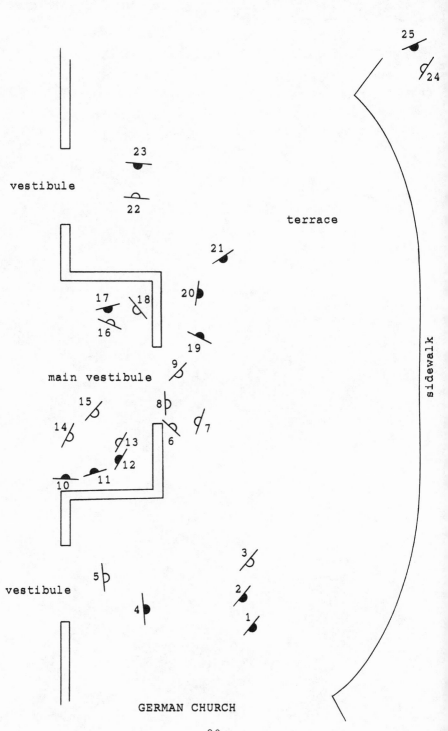

vestibule

terrace

main vestibule

vestibule

sidewalk

GERMAN CHURCH

90

Italian: Bar #6--Barone's

Barone's is located near Cermak and Western. There
were two waitresses, a middle aged woman in a gold uniform
and a woman in her early thirties in a white uniform. The
bartender was a man in his forties. There was a color
television to the right, behind the bar. Also behind the
bar were two plastic inflatable Pinocchio dolls. To the
left of the bar was another room which appeared to be a
dining room.

When we entered, the waitress in gold greeted us as if
we were welcomed strangers. She asked us if we wanted to go
into the dining room. We declined and stayed at the bar and
had our customary glass of beer.

There was a couple seated at a table across from the
left hand corner of the bar. The waitress in gold took a
seat at the table with them. This group spoke loudly and
fast, and the two women touched quite a bit. The young
waitress stood near the bar or sometimes in the doorway
between the bar and the dining room. Later, she sat at the
table next to the triad, watching television and
occasionally turning her head to contribute to the
conversation. The bartender stood behind the bar watching
television.

Later, a second couple arrived. They seated themselves
at the bar, greeted the other couple, and talked with the

bartender. The first couple left within moments, whereupon the waitress in gold got up and entered the conversation with the bartender and the recently arrived couple.

There was one notable measurement recorded during this visit. Again, as in the German bar, this involved an interaction strategy developed for a context in which a persons wished to divide attention between the television and the conversation. In this case it involved a cross-sex interaction. The observation was recorded on the sociofugal-sociopetal scale as a "5", the same as in the first German bar. This is the interaction described above involving the waitress in white.

Unlike the similar case in the German bar, the waitress did not seem to be disengaging herself but rather she seemed to have positioned herself in a way that facilitated her participation in two activities, without the total exclusion of either. We would suggest that position "5" on the sociofugal-sociopetal scale is not only a transitional phase moving toward disengagement from an interaction but also a position that allows the individual to participate simultaneously in two activities or interactions without committing herself fully to either interaction.

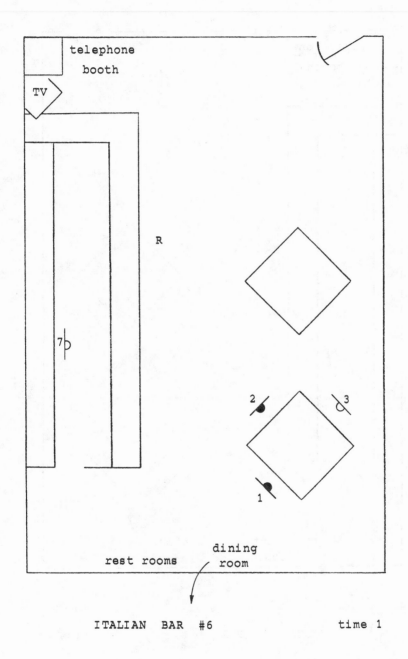

telephone
booth

TV

R

7

2

3

1

rest rooms

dining
room

ITALIAN BAR #6   time 1

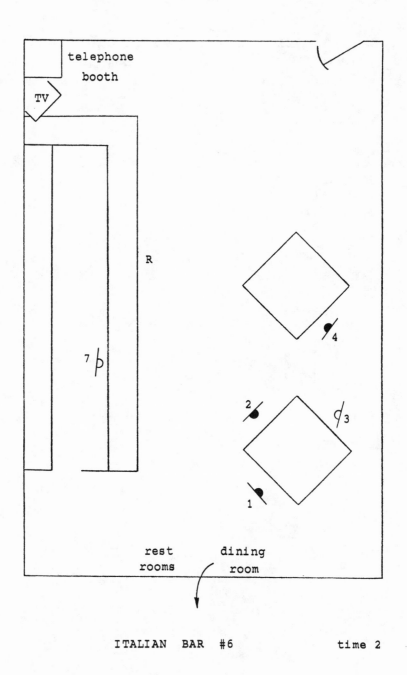

telephone
booth

TV

R

^{7}

^{2}
^{3}
^{4}
^{1}

rest
rooms

dining
room

ITALIAN BAR #6   time 2

94

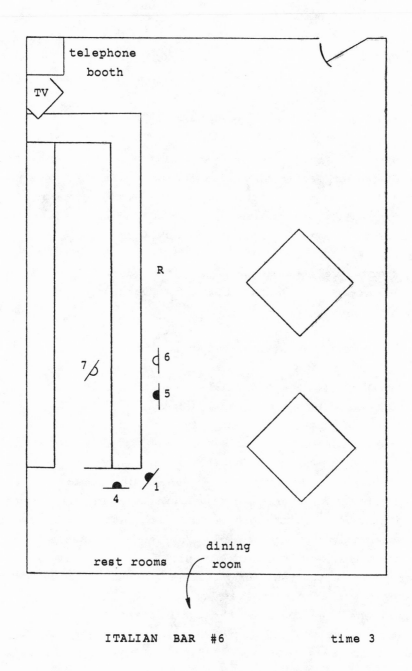

ITALIAN BAR #6   time 3

95

Italian: Bar #16--Barone's

Barone's was visited a second time as we were unable to locate another satisfactory Italian bar. The bartender and one of the waitresses, the older one, were present on this occasion. If they remembered us, they gave no clues. No other people from our first visit were present.

There were fourteen people in the bar when we entered. Shortly after taking the time one measures, four people departed.

At this visit six unusual observations were recorded, two at each time period. Three of these occurred within the kinesthetic (distance) code and involved cross-sex interactions with an old man being the central figure. In all three of these cases the old man was interacting with three women seated at a table. It should be noted, however, that although these observations are atypical for the Italian sample, they can be explained for the most part by the physical structuring of the furniture in the bar. In two of these cases the old man was interacting with two of the women across the table at which they were seated. And, in the third case the old man was seated at the bar and interacting with the woman closest to him.   (See map, persons 6 and 4, time three.) In the third interaction the old man was standing near the table and talking to a woman on the opposite side of the table.   All of their interactions were coded as "4's" on the kinesthetic scale.

96

In addition, we can see that marked cases were recorded in the touch code. Two of these observations were in cross-sex interactions among mates at time one (persons 10 - 11 and 12 - 13). Touching between persons 10 and 11 was coded as a "1" (holding) and between 12 and 13 as a "0" (prolonged holding or touching). The third case involved the old man and a young lady in her early twenties. This was recorded as a "0". We assume that the members of this dyad were related, since the old man referred to the girl's mother as a relative.

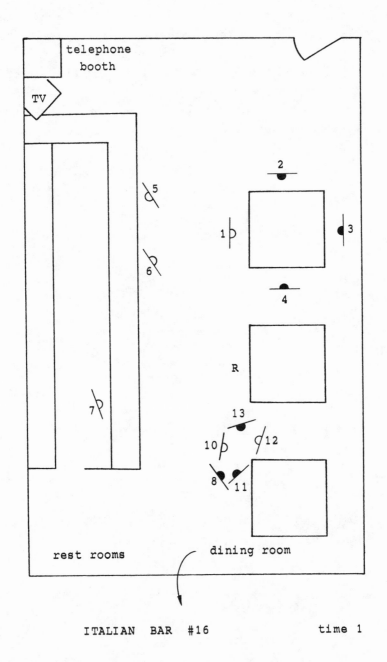

telephone booth

TV

rest rooms

dining room

ITALIAN BAR #16   time 1

98

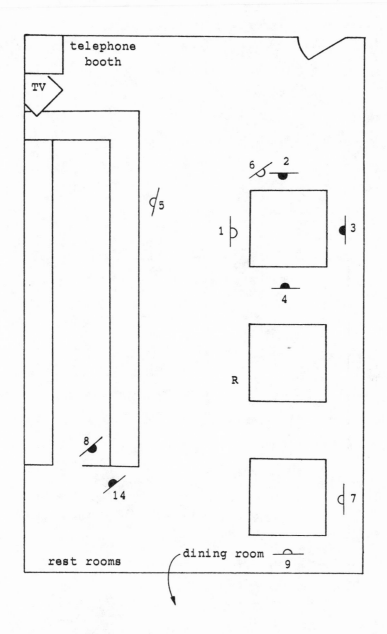

telephone booth

TV

rest rooms

dining room

ITALIAN BAR #16   time 2

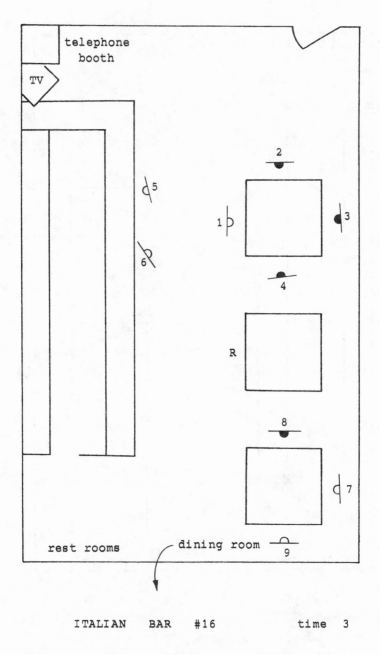

ITALIAN   BAR   #16   time   3

100

Italian: Church #26 -- St. Raphael

Our Italian community church was just around the corner
from Barone's.   Our experiences prior to and during the
service tend to support our judgment that we have sampled a
fairly tight knit Italian community.   The church is located
on a small residential street with multiple dwellings of
older construction. We had confounded our time schedule and
arrived ten minutes before a service was to begin instead of
right before a service was supposed to let out.   While
deciding what course of action to pursue we saw an older man
struggle to get out of his car and then fall down. We got
out of our car to help him up and were told by an observing
neighbor that he was both a drunk and a cripple.   By this
time several people were out on the street going to church
observing the scene.   We decided that since a number of
people had seen us on the street, we ought to attend the
service. As we went into the church a couple stopped us and
told us that the elderly man was a drunk.   It seemed that
people knew we were not from the neighborhood and that they
were in some way attempting to justify his and their own
behavior with regard to the situation.

The service was in Italian and one of us was helped by
an elderly woman to find the pages in the prayer book (to no
avail as the book was all in Italian).   The church was
fairly small with no real vestibule. Instead of a gathering
area inside of the church there was only an enclosed steep
set of stairs leading up to the sanctuary.   The stairs led

directly to the sidewalk where all of the interactions took place. Considering the fact that it was a rainy day, it seemed a bit amazing that there were any sustained interactions at all.

We found marked cases on the touch measure and some interesting cases on the position measure. The three instances of holding we found were easily explained: 1) cross-sex, 2) same sex female, 3) same sex male juvenile.

Once again we found no adult male holding, but a high propensity for spot touching. The only non-vertical positions we found in any of the churches were recorded here when we observed two young boys sitting on a ledge outside of the church (since they were not sitting with feet touching the ground, we coded them as if they were on bar stools). Inasmuch as many of the other churches we sampled had numerous stone ledges and walls to sit on, it is significant that only in the small, homey Italian neighborhood were these utilized for sitting.

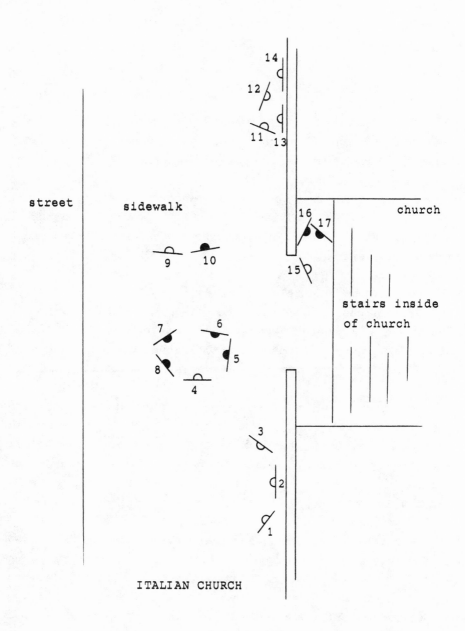

street

sidewalk

church

14

12

11   13

16   17

15

9   10

stairs inside
of church

7   6

8   5

4

3

2

1

ITALIAN CHURCH

103

Serbian: Bars #7 and #17--Serbian Club

The Serbian Club is housed in an old building on the
near north side close to Milwaukee Avenue and Division
Street. Alongside the bar is a restaurant. Although the
bar and the restaurant are in the same building, the
restaurant is, in a sense, in another world since the
restaurant is a tourist attraction having a separate
entrance from that leading into the bar. The bar also had a
second side entrance.

All of the clientele in the restaurant were dressed up,
the men in coats and ties, the women in dresses, while in
the bar the men were in casual dress or work clothes. None
of the restaurant patrons entered through the bar, and none
of the bar patrons entered through the restaurant.

The restaurant half of the aging structure had been
renovated, but the bar obviously had not. The barroom was
in poor condition: the bar was old and warped in places;
the liquor cabinets retained their original doors with
leaded glass window panes. There was a television, in use,
and a jukebox.

Both the restaurant and bar seemed to be a family
operation. On the second visit the man who had been the
maitre d' on the first visit tended bar. The man's wife was
the waitress in the restaurant. Also, the Serbian Club was
in a residential area with a "mom and pop" grocery across

the street.

Both Serbian samples were taken at this establishment. Other Serbian establishments were investigated, but none proved satisfactory, as the others were tourist attractions and lacked any Serbian clientele. The bar at the Serbian Club, in contrast, was a neighborhood establishment. All the patrons, with a few exceptions, spoke Serbian, we assume. These exceptions were four adolescent males who spoke English and Spanish. The other exceptions were a black man and a black woman who purchased beer and, after a few minutes of conversation with the bartender, departed with their purchases. These exceptions were excluded from the coding.

One outstanding case was observed on the sociofugal and sociopetal code. This was recorded as a "5". As in the Italian bar, one of the interactants was facing the television and making comments over his shoulder to the other member of the dyad.

An observation made during the first visit illustrates a difficulty with the sociofugal and sociopetal code as defined by Hall (1963: 1008-1009). This difficulty occurs at position "4". Hall says that the subjects are positioned "side by side with the north-south axis running through parallel to their shoulders . . ." (1963: 1008), (see definitions of codes). In Hall's graphic display of the sociofugal and sociopetal code the north-south axis runs through shoulder axes of both subjects. Several instances were recorded in which one subject was behind the other, to one side, and yet parallel. This configuration establishes a spatial arrangement and interaction pattern similar to that of the sociofugal and sociopetal position coded as a "5", since verbal communication and eye contact must take place over one participant's shoulder. The weakness lies in the attempt to code a two dimensional spatial relation with a one dimensional system.

Although Hall does not consider a "4" on the sociofugal and sociopetal as sociofugal, it would seem, in cases like that above, that a "4" in such a spatial arrangement would be sociofugal. It should be made clear, however, that unlike position "5" on sociofugal and sociopetal scale, a "4" in such a spatial arrangement should not be viewed as a transition into disengagement. In either position "4" or "5", it is possible for one or both of the interactants to divide their attention. For example, an interaction within a triad involving two individuals in this position would result in a division of attention for two of those involved. In position "5" two interactants may be viewing or engaged in separate activities, yet still be an integral part of the conversation. So several interaction strategies are employed in special settings, that cannot be accurately recorded with Hall's code.

One marked case was recorded. This involved the same cross-sex dyad referred to above. The touch score for this interaction was coded as a "1", the only "1" recorded in the Serbian example. In the contingency table two "1's" are recorded, since each interactant receives a separate coding.

No marked or unusual cases on any of the measures were observed during the second visit.

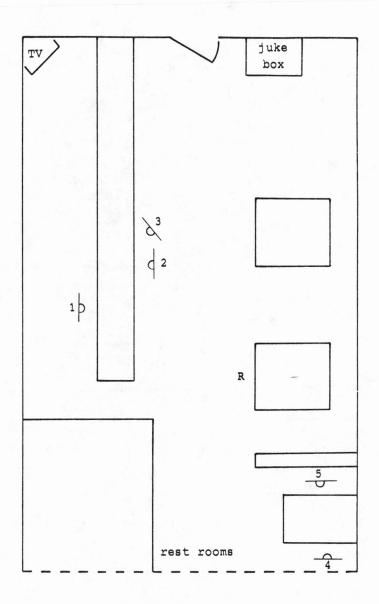

TV

juke
box

3

2

1

R

5

rest rooms

4

SERBIAN BAR #7   time 1

107

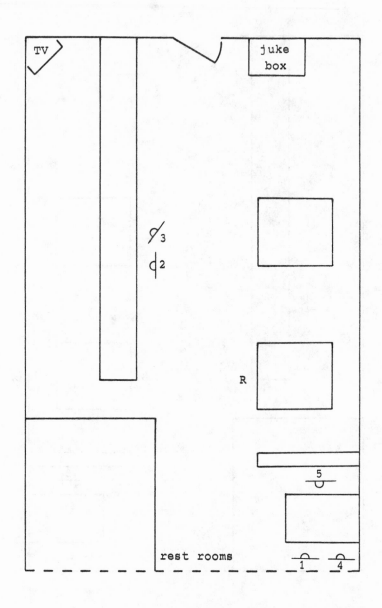

SERBIAN   BAR   #7   time 2

108

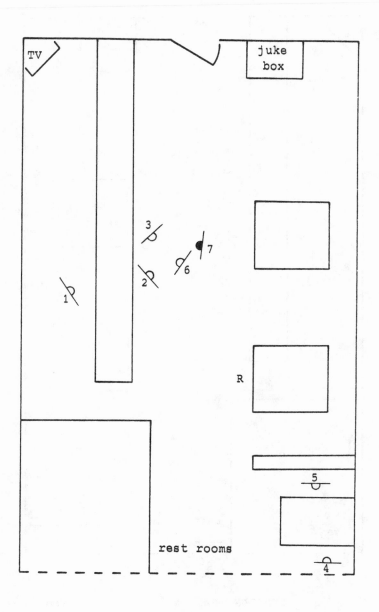

SERBIAN   BAR   #7   time 3

109

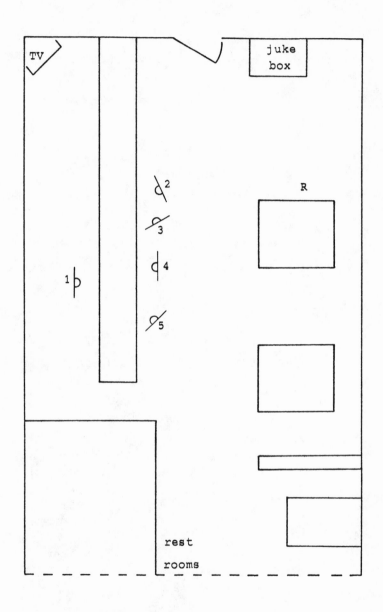

TV

juke
box

R

2

3

1

4

5

rest

rooms

SERBIAN BAR #17   time 1

110

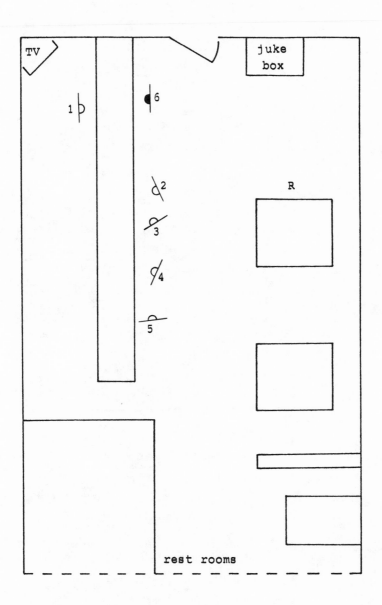

TV

juke
box

1

6

2

3

4

5

R

rest rooms

SERBIAN BAR #17   time 2

111

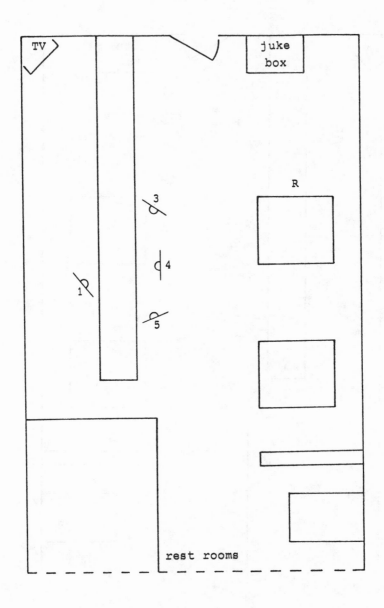

SERBIAN BAR #17   time 3

112

Serbian: Church #27 -- St. Gregory

The Serbian church we selected was only three blocks
from our Mexican church.   It stood on the corner of two
quiet residential streets surrounded by single family
dwellings.   St. Gregory's is on a small lot and is of very
recent construction. Surrounding the church is a chain link
fence which gave the grounds a private, monastic quality.
The parishioners were a tightly knit group with everyone
well acquainted with one another.   This factor, along with
the presence of the chain link fence, made us feel that our
presence would be most obtrusive if we were to enter the
church grounds.   But, since the sidewalk is very close to
the outdoor interaction space we hoped to observe, we had no
trouble coding the information.   An older building on the
northwest side of the lot is used as a social hall for
refreshment after the service.   The small area between the
buildings served as a communal location where those on their
way to the social hall gathered to interact.   Three large
communicating groups were observed; a loosely knit crowd was
directly in front of the church's main entrance where a good
deal of the available space was used to socialize.   In the
enclosed area, space was fairly limited, which helps to
account for the narrow range of distance observed (See
contingency table for kinesthetic).

Once again the only prolonged touching recorded was
between two women in a direct face-to-face interaction.   The
Serbians were also observed to have the most direct eye

contact, which correlates with their higher rate of direct
shoulder axis when compared with the other groups.

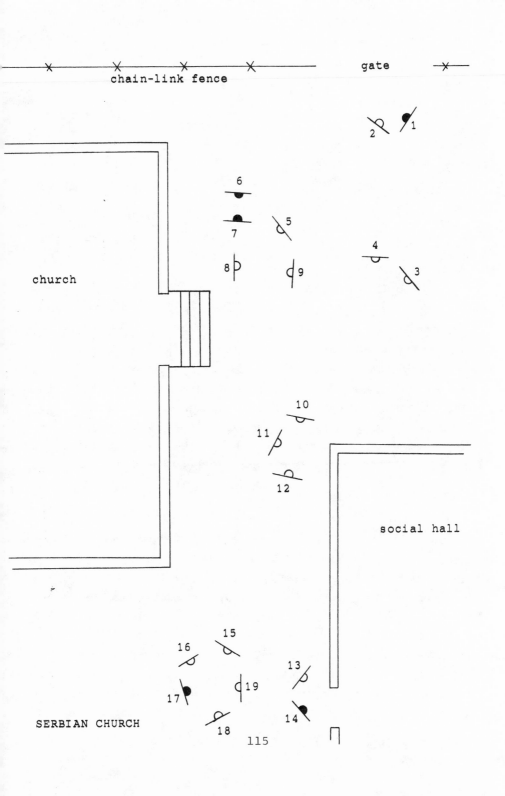

chain-link fence

gate

church

social hall

SERBIAN CHURCH

115

Irish: Bar #18 -- Finnerty's

On the south side of Chicago near the intersection of
63rd and Kedzie are numerous bars bearing Irish names. This
neighborhood was selected for our sample of Irish bars.

Finnerty's is on Kedzie a few blocks north of 63rd.
Physically the bar is not the least bit remarkable. At the
left end of the room, behind the bar, is a color television.
 Behind the bar is displayed the latest in slick bar ad art,
the type with changing idyllic scenes. Below the ad art, on
top of the liquor cabinet, is a tropical fish tank. On a
table across from the bar was a carton full of pound cakes
which were for sale. Three men were seated at the right end
of the bar. Next to them were two male-female couples that
formed a "with". A few stools to their left was a single
male. Most of the clientele appeared to be in their
forties.

In this bar, as in the second Irish bar, we were
requested to show identification. The bartender, unlike the
one in the Polish bar, seemed interested in our ages rather
than using the identifications as an excuse to refuse us
service.

After the time one measures were taken, two members of
the "with" at the right end of the bar exited. The
remaining person was joined by a newcomer before the time
three measures were taken. Also, between times two and

116

three another man entered and joined the "single" to the left of the foursome. This man was the interactant who produced the anomalous cases in this bar and the only instances where reparative action was required in the entire study.

The man in question was rather atypical for the clientele in Finnerty's. He had a swarthy complexion, and his voice loudness was the highest in this bar; a "4" was recorded (louder than normal). Also, he was the only man in this bar to engage in male-male spot touching (though this was noted in the other Irish bars). Other instances of spot touching occurred in two cross-sex dyads and one female-female dyad.

The ruddy complexioned fellow continually decreased the distance between himself and the other interactant in this dyad. The other interactant attempted to regain control of the situation. He backed off as each violation of space occurred. Another normative violation was also noted. The man in question was reprimanded by the bartender on several occasions for his use of billingsgate. Undoubtedly the bartender felt that this was inappropriate since three women were within earshot -- the two women coded and the daughter of a gentleman who was not coded.

This gentleman last mentioned and his seventeen year old daughter were not coded because they were interacting with one of the investigators. Information regarding the neighborhood was gathered from this conversation. It seems that this neighborhood is mixed Irish and Lithuanian. The investigators feel that it is safe to assume that the atypical gentleman, mentioned earlier, was Lithuanian; this would account for some of his anomalous behavior and his unwelcome reception in this bar.

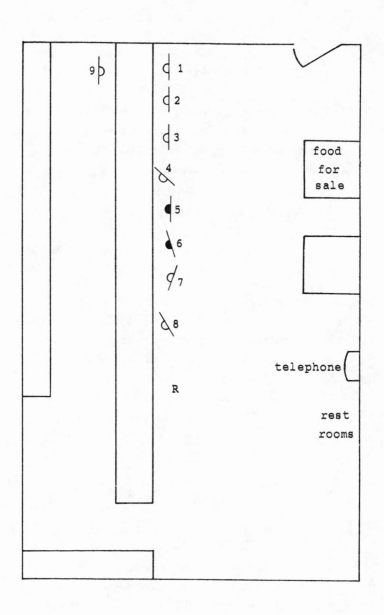

IRISH BAR #18   time 1

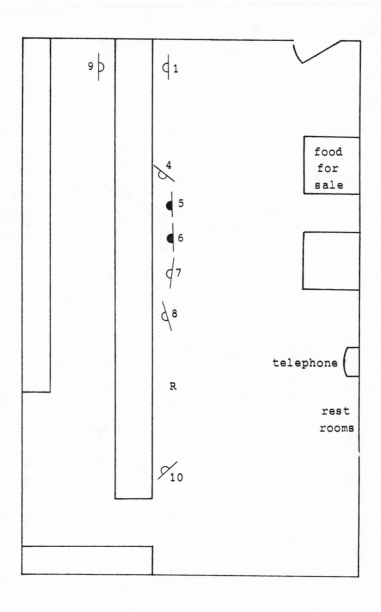

IRISH   BAR   #18   time 2

119

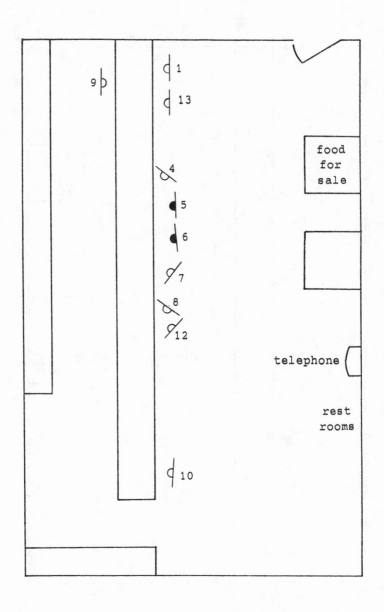

IRISH BAR #18   time 3

Irish: Bar #8 -- The Blarney Stone

The Blarney Stone, though by no means plush, provides a more up-scale atmosphere than Finnerty's.   This bar seems to have been recently decorated.   Bar ad art of a European variety--advertisements for Guinnes Stout and Harp Ale-- replaced the slick bar ad art noted in the previous bar.   A color television was in use, and a jukebox was played occasionally.   The television was above the doorway leading to a room with tables and chairs.   On the wall was a map of Ireland.   Guinness Stout was served on tap, and a copy of the Irish News on top of the liquor cabinet could be perused by interested customers.   As in the other Irish bars, the cabinet displayed several brands of Irish whiskey including Bushmills and Tullamore Dew.

To the right of the bar, in the back room, was a small kitchen.   At one point during our visit,   a customer went into the kitchen and began cooking a hot dog and soup.   When he ran into some difficulty in preparing the soup, he called to the bartender for assistance.

All of the interaction took place at the corner of the bar nearest the entrance.   Most of the men were in their fifties, with the exception of the bartender and the man who prepared the snack.   All, except the bartender, seemed to have had their spirits enhanced by the spirits proffered. As a result of the merriment, nearly half of the vocal codings were "4's" (very loud).   The bartender spoke in a normal or soft tone of voice. A few of the kinesthetic scores were coded as "10's", but most were "20's" or greater. In spite of the merriment and the small distances between interactants, the only cases of touching observed were accidental. No other touching occurred. In more than half of the observations made, no touching was noted ("4" on the touch scale).

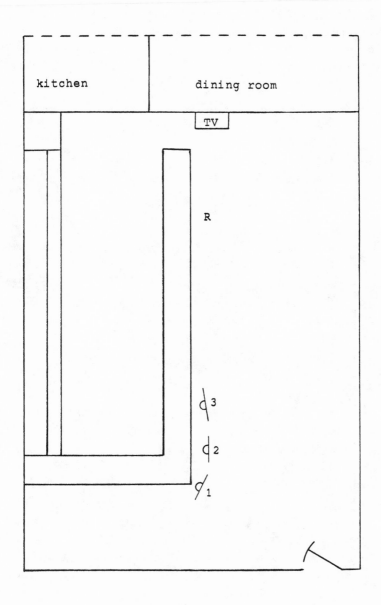

IRISH BAR #8   time 1

123

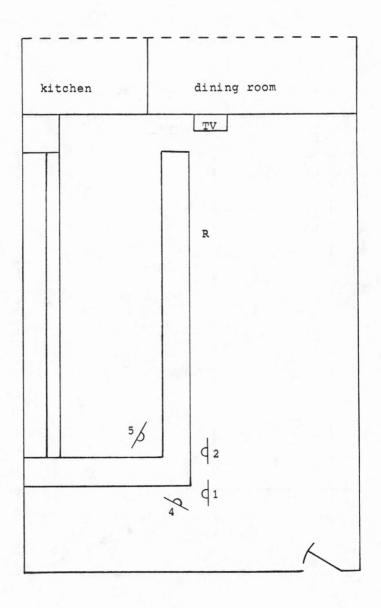

kitchen

dining room

TV

R

5

2

1

4

IRISH   BAR   #8   time 2

124

Irish: Bar #13 -- Gallaher's

The third Irish bar had a much younger crowd than the two other Irish bars. Most of the clientele were in their late twenties and early thirties. Gallahers was the plushest of the three Irish bars, with carpeted floors and wood paneling. Again, a map of Ireland was on the wall. Guinness Stout was served on tap, and the usual stock of Irish whiskey was on display. The sandwiches served were heated in an electronic oven. Again we found a color television, but this one was not in use. We were not asked for identification.

Three customers were playing pool, but they were not coded as they were out of our view except when each took his shot. The room which housed the pool table was separate from the bar. After each pool player finished his turn, he took a seat behind a partition out of our view.

Unlike the other Irish bars, two of the three tables were used. A male-female dyad sat at a table at right angles to each other. At the other table four men were seated. The use of tables accounts for the varied sociofugal sociopetal scores when compared with the other Irish bars. In the first Irish bar the "0's" were coded with a bartender interacting across the bar. No "1's" and four "2's" were recorded in the first Irish bar.

In Gallaher's we find the bartender interacting across

the bar, which accounts for some of the "0's" recorded. The
other "0's" occurred within the group of four seated at the
table at all three times. The preponderance of "1's" and
"2's" recorded in the last two Irish bars can be accounted
for by the use of the corner of the bar and the use of
tables in these bars. This was not the case in the first
Irish bar. Although the bar was crowded, there were enough
seats to accommodate those seated at the tables. It seems
that several customers selected tables as their preferred
location, since several stools remained at the bar.

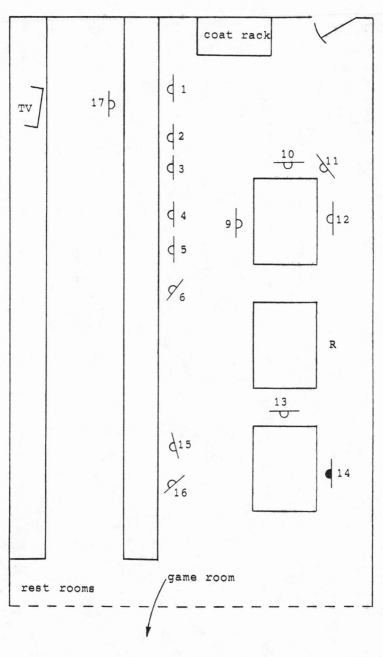

coat rack

TV

17

1

2

3

4

5

6

10 11

9 12

R

13

15

14

16

rest rooms

game room

IRISH   BAR   #13   time 1

127

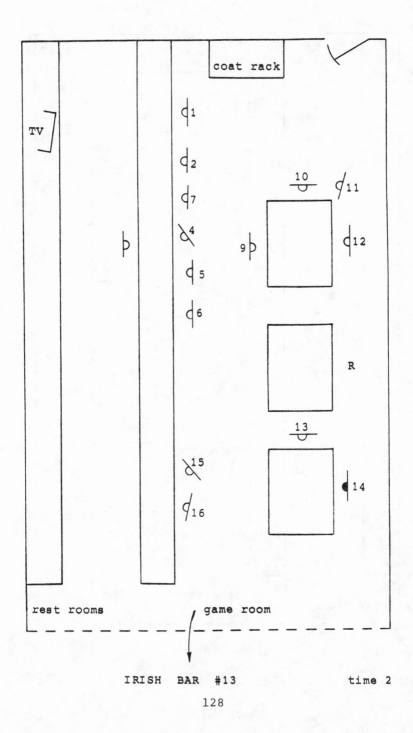

IRISH   BAR #13   time 2

128

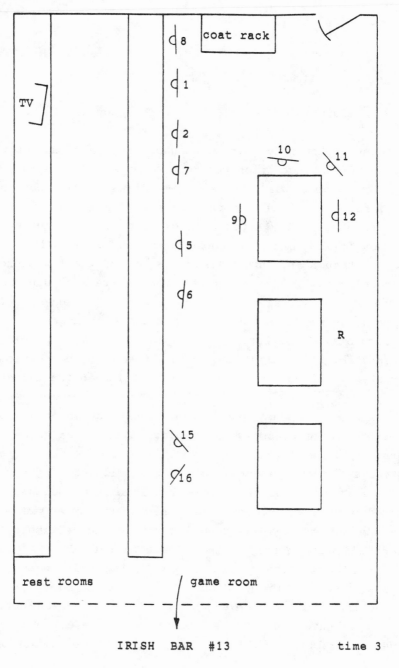

coat rack

TV

8

1

2

7

10   11

9   12

5

6

R

15

16

rest rooms   game room

IRISH   BAR   #13   time 3

129

Irish: Church #28 -- St. Christopher's

Many of the city's Irish neighborhoods have dissipated, leaving no distinct Irish residential area. Unlike the bars to which people will travel some distance for community relations, the churchgoer prefers the corner church of his newer neighborhood. After much difficulty and conversation with an Irish family we chose a church on the far south side. Although St. Christopher's is one of the few churches in the city still giving jig lessons, we are most dubious as to the Irish heritage of the parishioners observed. This sample is probably our weakest in terms of homogeneity, but it accurately reflects the rapidly changing residence patterns of the city and a St. Patty's day cultural stereotype: anyone in green is a bit Irish in their heart.

The church is of recent stone construction in a middle to upper middle class neighborhood. There were three main doors, each with its own small vestibule. The main vestibule was at the north end of the building. Newspapers were being sold in this area by a middle aged man who entered into none but the most necessary conversations. Only one interaction was recorded within the vestibule, the others all took place on the sidewalks outside. A priest (number 17) was observed talking with two older women just outside the vestibule doors. No direct face-to-face interactions were observed in this fairly nonstructured space. We have one notable case on voice level in a cross gender interaction inside the vestibule. Here a middleaged

130

woman (number 11) wearing a mink cape was especially loud when talking to her male partners. Once again, the Irish were observed to touch least and stand farthest apart when compared with interactions in the other churches.

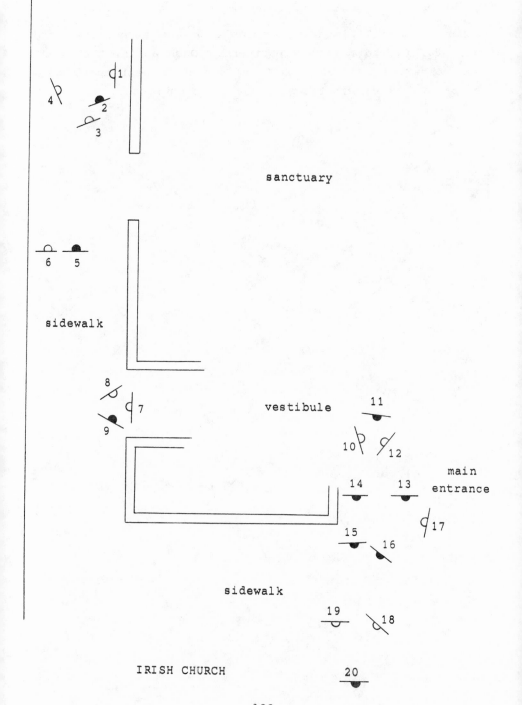

sanctuary

6   5

sidewalk

8
  7
9

vestibule   11

                10   12

                        main
                      entrance

            14   13

            15
                16   17

sidewalk

            19   18

IRISH CHURCH   20

132

American: Bar #9 -- The Red Plume

Both American bars are in Skokie, a suburb north of Chicago.   In terms of setting, there are outstanding differences between the two.   The first bar is on Dempster Avenue.   The Red Plume, as it is called, is rather spacious in comparison with the other bars studied.   Opposite the bar are several booths with an area of twenty feet or so separating them from the bar.   Against one wall is a piano bar.   A drum set and public address equipment were stacked behind the bar.   The space age jukebox was used; most of the selections played were country and western tunes.   All of the patrons, with the exception of two men seated in a booth, were at the bar.   Most of the men were attired in business suits.

The walls of the bar were decorated with model sailing ships, portraits of clowns, fish nets, pieces of driftwood, and a swordfish mounted on one of the walls.   The floor was carpeted, with the exception of a ten by fifteen foot dance floor opposite the piano bar.   Generally the decor was tacky.

The bartender was female, and there were two barmaids. All of the customers, with the exception of one, were male.

Three unusual cases on the kinesthetic code were observed.   The first was a marked case of cross-sex touching.   This dyad was recorded as a "1" (within body contact distance on the kinesthetic scale). More important, their touch score was recorded as a "0" (prolonged or extended holding). This couple was dancing.

The other marked cases involved the bartender and two male patrons at time three. In the first dyad, the distance was recorded as "4" (within reaching distance). The second was recorded as "40" (just outside reaching distance). In both cases the bartender was recorded as speaking in a very loud tone of voice, a "4" on the vocal scale, while the other interactants were recorded as a "1" (very soft) and a "2" (soft).

At time two the bartender and the first of the two men mentioned above were engaged in an interaction at a distance of "4", and the bartender's vocal was recorded as a "4" (very loud) again, while the man had a vocal score of "3" (loud). In this setting, the bartender has the prerogative to set the tone of interaction, even if it deviates from the norm.

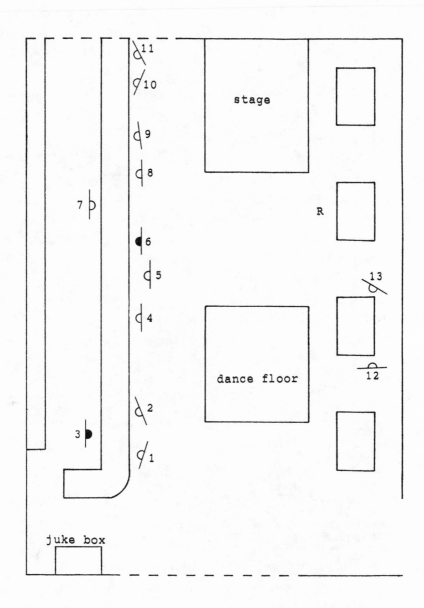

stage

R

13

dance floor

12

7

6

5

4

2

3

1

11

10

9

8

juke box

AMERICAN BAR #9   time 1

135

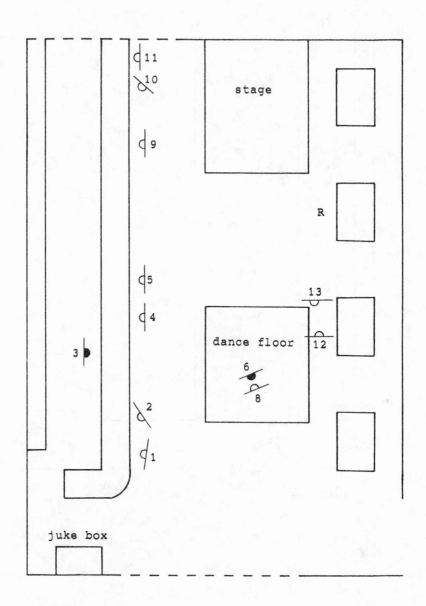

stage

R

13

dance floor

12

6

8

3

5

4

2

1

11

10

9

juke box

AMERICAN   BAR   #9   time   2

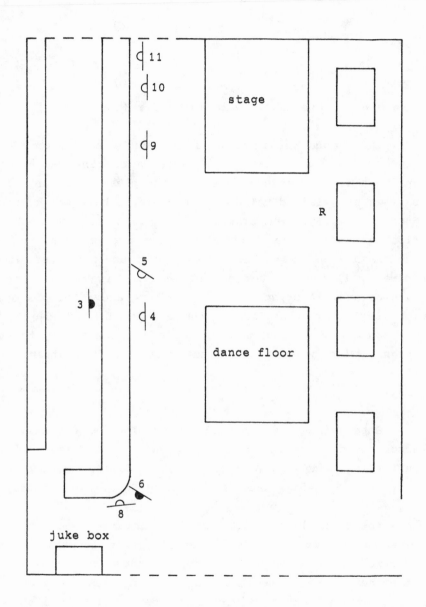

AMERICAN BAR #9   time 3

American: Bar #19 -- The Mallorca

The second bar is about a mile and a half from The Red
Plume.   The bar is part of a restaurant.   The decor, quite
unlike that of The Red Plume, was the plushest of any of the
bars we had visited.   The liquor cabinets have carved wooden
doors in a Spanish style.   The walls are covered with
flocked paper.   The lighting fixtures are wrought iron with
Guadalajara Glass.   The walls are also decorated with a
framed bullfight poster and contrasting framed Currier and
Ives prints.   A crystal chandelier hung above the piano bar.
The bar was padded, as was the one in The Red Plume.   The
bar stools were four-legged captain's chairs of barstool
height, with seats that do not swivel.   The bartender was
male and was assisted by a waitress in a very revealing
playsuit.

Entertainment was provided by a black male vocalist who
accompanied himself on the piano.   A female patron,
fulfilling all of the stereotypes, called to the piano
player: "You sing just like Nat King Cole.   That's good."

In both bars, all of the interactions that had
kinesthetic scores of "2" (one forearm's length) or less,
occurred in a cross-sex pair.   Four marked cases on the
kinesthetic code were observed.   In the first case a cross-
sex dyad was seated at the piano bar, and the kinesthetic
score was recorded as a "10".   In this case we find that
there is holding within this cross-sex dyad.   The other

138

three are unusual cases involving one principal interactant
-- a thin, sportily attired, middle-aged woman. At time two
she was interacting with the barmaid and the bartender. The
kinesthetic score for both dyads was recorded as a "40"
(just outside reaching distance). The woman's vocal score
was a "4" (very loud) in both cases, and the barmaid's vocal
was also a "4". The bartender's vocal score was recorded as
a "2" (just below normal) in his interaction with the thin
woman. His calm tone and mildly disapproving facial
expressions imparted the message to the women that their
loud remarks were on his margins of acceptability for that
setting.

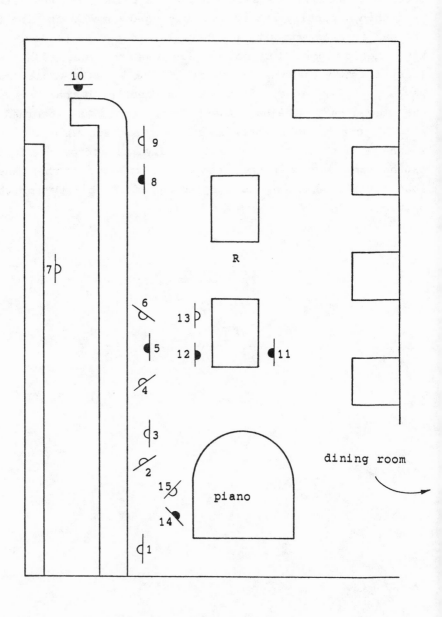

AMERICAN   BAR   #19   time 1

140

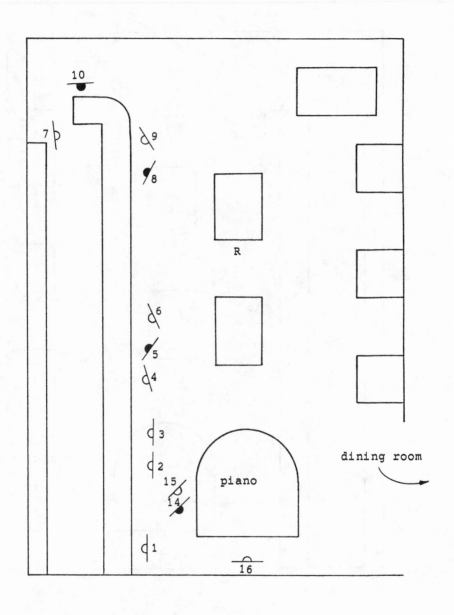

AMERICAN   BAR   #19   time 2

141

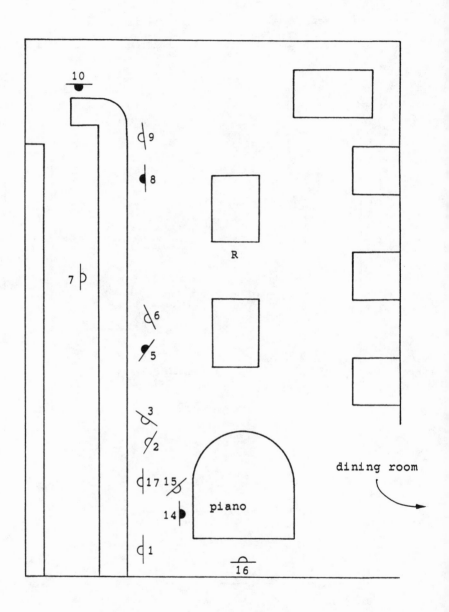

10

9

8

7

6

5

3
2

17 15

14   piano

1

R

dining room

16

AMERICAN   BAR   #19   time 3
142

American: Church #29 -- St. Mary's

We chose the northern suburb of Skokie to sample an
American Catholic church. The church is located one block
from a boulevard and is sided on the north by a large, well
groomed park. The surrounding homes are of 1950's construction and of the middle and upper middle class variety. St.
Mary's is of stone and wood beam construction and is a
fairly large structure as compared with other churches in
our sample. There is a spacious parking lot to the east
(this being our only church with enough extra land for
parishioner parking). The parking lot was full of cars and
it was along its margins that many of our coded
post-service interactions took place. There were three
main entrances to the vestibule: one opening directly to
the front and down a short flight of steps, the other two
being at each side (one to the parking lot and the other to
the sidewalk on the west). The vestibule was not deep, but
wide in comparison to the church's width, with an extended
covering over the stairs that created a larger protected
area. Newspapers were being sold under this overhang by
two teenagers (Numbers 15 and 17 on the map).

Interactions were very short and fleeting, much the
same as with the German church. The only sustained interactions were inside the vestibule between two women and a
young child, all of possible Mexican extraction. This triad
also served as an outstanding case for sociofugal and socio-

petal. As with most sustained meetings, the shoulder axis assumed is more face-to-face. The only other direct axis taken was between two teenagers (male and female, the boy being one of our entrepreneurs) who also serve as an unusual case for this sample. In comparison with the other churches, the form of touching that took place at St. Mary's was particularly notable. Here we found much cross-sex spot touching of the arm in arm variety. In none of the other churches was this courtly manner observed. Once again, because of the limitations of Hall's code, we were able to distinguish such specific types of touching only in our ethnographic accounts and not in our quantified summaries.

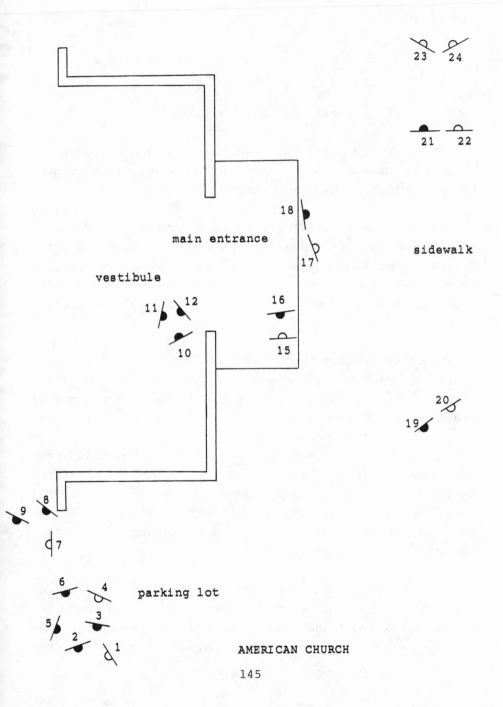

main entrance

sidewalk

vestibule

parking lot

AMERICAN CHURCH

145

Greek: Bar #10 --- Plakos'

The bar selected for part of the Greek sample is located on Halstead near a Greek pastry shop, Greek grocery stores, and other Greek restaurants.

Plakos' seems primarily to be a tourist attraction. That is, we saw what appeared to be a great number of non-Greeks in the dining room. There were, however, several men at the bar, all of whom spoke Greek. The bartender spoke and often sang in Greek. The rest of the staff also spoke Greek.

When we entered the bar the men reacted to the female member of the team. Whenever she would look in their direction, all eyes turned to her. These were not merely seductive glances but licentious leers.

Most of the interaction was within a triad and sometimes across the bar with the bartender or one of the waitresses who was cutting meat from the racks of lamb. There was another man who did not speak to anyone, but he did indulge in gazing at the female member of the team whenever he got the chance.

Unlike the other places we visited, the bar did not seem to be the main source of business. There were two large dining rooms that were filled to near capacity. The bar was a small section partitioned off from one of the

146

dining rooms.

The fourth man, who had not been interacting, left the bar by the time we made our observations at time two. The bartender came out from behind the bar and sat at this man's seat.

Moments before making the observations at time three, a couple with two children entered and began interacting with the group of four at the bar. It was at this time that we observed marked cases of touching, but these can be explained by age and sex differences in the participants, with one exception. The man (#9, at time three) was holding his son's hand (#12, at time three). The woman (#10, at time three) also held the son's hand, and she also was touching her daughter (#11, at time three).

The instance of holding that doesn't fit the age and sex difference explanation occurred with the same man and one of the men in the trio first mentioned (#1, at time three). These men had their arms about each other's shoulders; their shoulder axis was coded as a "3".

It is interesting to note that the man and woman who entered last spoke in a normal tone of voice to the men at the bar, while the men spoke to them in a very loud tone of voice. Also, while the man and woman spoke loudly to the children, the children responded in a normal tone of voice. The age differential is thus consistently coded in distinctions of voice loudness, with the senior participant in an interaction in each instance speaking louder. Prior to the entrance of the couple and their children, most of the interactions took place in a loud or very loud tone of voice, and Greek was the language spoken.

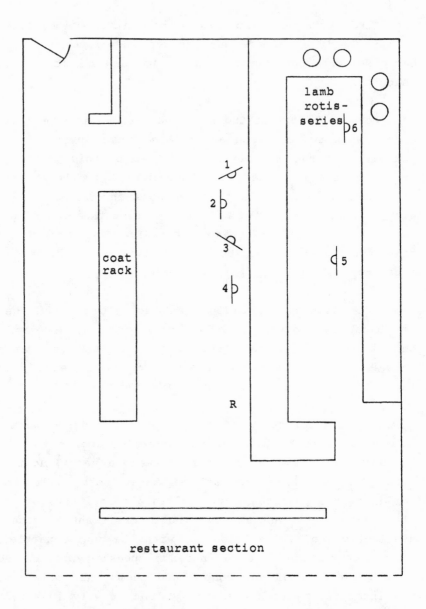

coat
rack

lamb
rotis-
series

1
2
3
4
5
6

R

restaurant section

GREEK   BAR   #10   time 1

148

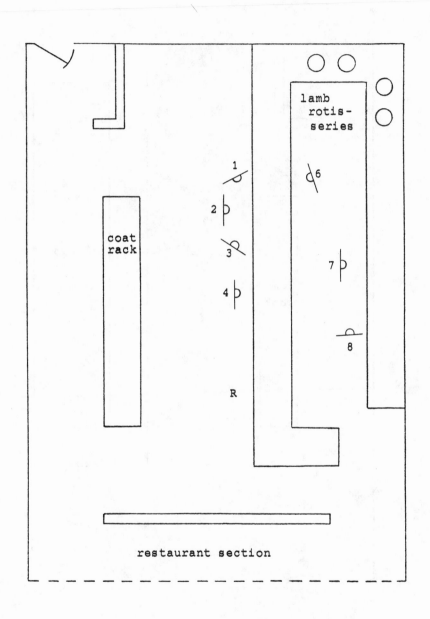

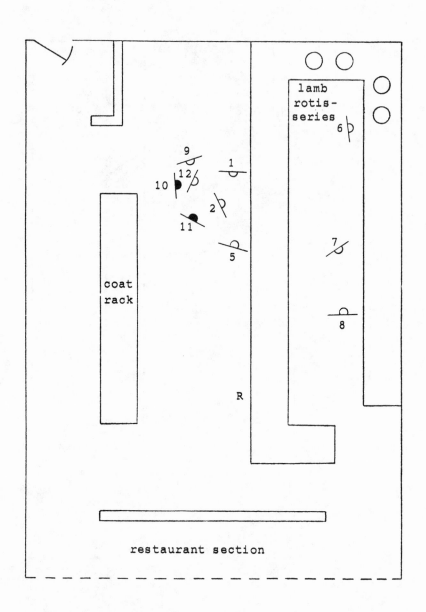

lamb
rotis-
series

9

12
10

1

2

11

5

6

7

8

coat
rack

R

restaurant section

GREEK   BAR   #10   time 3

Greek: Bar #20 -- The Corinthian

The Corinthian is a dimly lit bar a few blocks down the street from the first Greek bar studied. The bar is partitioned off from the rest of the room which was neatly arranged with tables and chairs. Behind the bar and to the left, as one faces the liquor cabinet, is a statue of Venus. On the opposite wall is a mural of maidens in diaphanous gowns frolicking in Greek ruins.

Four men, including the bartender, were clustered at the right hand corner of the bar, near the entrance. They drank beer and talked with one another; the conversation was in Greek. Although the pitch variation in their speech was quite noticeable, they spoke for the most part in a normal tone of voice.

Frequently the bartender would look over at us, and the man closest to us would occasionally glance over also. Three of the men were in their fifties, and the other seemed to be in his late twenties. When we left, the bartender bid us "good night".

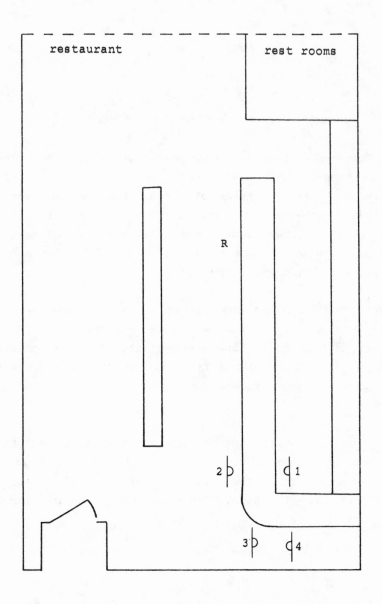

restaurant

rest rooms

R

2 | | 1

3 | | 4

GREEK   BAR   #20   time 1

152

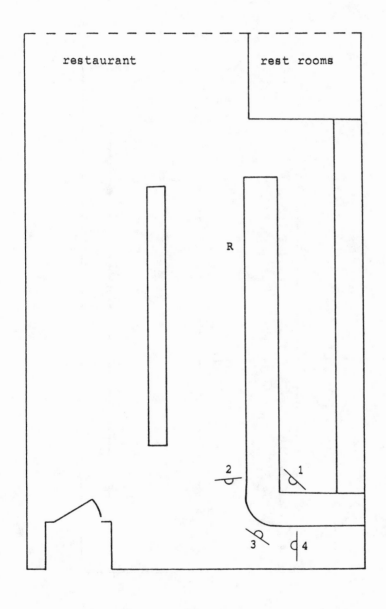

restaurant   rest rooms

R

2   1

3   4

GREEK   BAR   #20   time 2

153

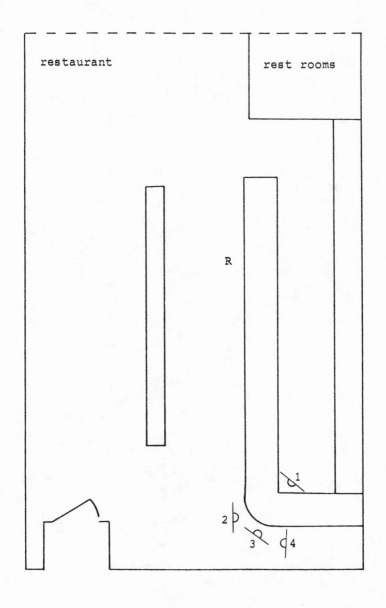

restaurant

rest rooms

R

1

2

3

4

GREEK   BAR   #20   time 3

154

Greek: Church #30 -- St. Anthony

For our Greek sample we chose a Greek orthodox church to the west of the Greek neighborhood.   St. Anthony's was an imposing stone structure facing a main boulevard.   The sidewalks in front were extremely large (20 ft.), and buses ran regularly along the main boulevard.   There was a fairly long steep stairway with a metal rail climbing up to the church's entryway.   At the top of the stairs was a small cement area leading to the three sets of doors.   It was here that one of our marked case interactions took place.

The most atypical interaction pattern in all of our Greek samples was an instance of very distant spacing that took place in front of these doors.   To avoid being hit by the door the dyad was forced to stand at a distance allowing no possible contact (A "5" on the kinesthetic scale).   This is an obviously aberrant communication style related to the fixed and semi-fixed space, since none of the other Greek parishoners selected interaction distance in the four intervening cells (03 - 30 - 04 - 40).   Inside the door at the top of the stairs was a large vestibule with a candle seller and his table of wares.   There were also stairs in the vestibule leading down to a social hall that was utilized after the three hour service for refreshments.

Interesting marked cases were found in two dyads on the touch code.   One was between two women in their sixties. The other was an old woman grabbing a young girl while

155

maneuvering the steep steps outside the church. The teenage
girl did not reciprocate the older woman's touching. We
found this same form of marked interaction in our Polish
church. (An old woman holding onto a young woman with the
young woman assisting.) We also found Hall's code to be
inadequate when we coded a woman who was yelling at the
voice level "4". Her decibel level was considerably greater
than any other people we coded as "4s".

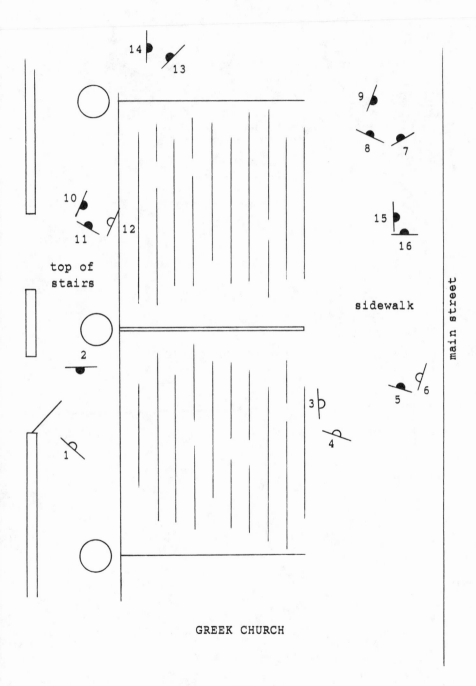

top of
stairs

sidewalk

main street

GREEK CHURCH

157

III

ANALYSIS AND COMPARISON OF ETHNIC INTERACTIONS

Analysis and Comparison of Ethnic Interactions

At the time this study was begun the only published application of Hall's coding system was Watson's analysis (1970), which constitutes an expansion of his original project conducted at the University of Colorado (Watson and Graves 1966). His study was carried out along the lines of the classical psychological experiment utilizing foreign and American students as subjects in a controlled laboratory situation. In contrast, this study has proceeded along lines of naturalistic observation involving a much larger sample but measuring fewer points in time per individual.

Whereas all of Watson's subjects were originally of diverse national origins (and an admittedly biased student sample), the 'subjects' observed in the present study were all of one overall population, the city of Chicago. Since Chicago is so well known for its diverse ethnic populations, the authors have assumed that any differences in the proxemic action of the sample groups, would surface in the measurement of their interaction strategies. The null hypothesis would be that there are no significant differences between ethnic groups; all groups act essentially the same in a proxemic sense. To test this, the researchers have applied the chi-square test and the Kruskal-Wallis test, where appropriate. These measures of statistical significance indicate if such differences are actually present and, if so, at what level of significance the differences exist. By looking at the individual test statistics and the expected cell frequencies between groups (see data sheets), the point at which these differences occur and their associated magnitude can be assessed. In a parallel manner any similarities which may exist in the proxemic patterns of the various groups should be traceable.

The data analysis has been conducted on a number of different levels, to help specify the nature of the differences noted in the contingency tables. The first table following each measure indicates the raw frequency scores for each bar on all levels considered (i.e., time x measure, bar x measure, and combined bar x measure, for each ethnic group). The second contingency table presents the observed over expected frequencies on three distinct levels: bar, church, and group.[10] Finally, the graphs allow a comparison of percentage scores for each group on bar (combined) and church levels. The data has also been compared by sex and by gender-paired dyads (male-male, female-female, and male-female). The results of these levels are discussed only when they appear to be significant and add meaningfully to the analysis. All such cross-sex and within-sex comparisons were necessarily made only on the church data. In this setting adequate male and female samples were obtainable for all ethnic groups. Substantial samples of gender-specific actions were not always available in the bars, since women were often absent from this par-ticular setting.

Unfortunately Watson did not utilize the non-parametric techniques of this study, but rather applied the standard "T test" which is not appropriate for the type of data under consideration.[11] Only two of the measures, kinesthetic and sociofugal-sociopetal, are at all amenable to such a test, and even these would require some manipulation prior to application of the "T test." The inapplicability of the "T test" to the data rests on the fact that all measures, with the exception of the above two, are of the nominal sort.

The kinesthetic and sociofugal-sociopetal measures are of the ordinal variety, though exhibiting some interval characteristics. As Seigal notes, the "T test" requires data of at least the interval sort (1956: 19). Since none of the measures meet this standard to the researchers' satisfaction, the weaker, but more appropriate chi-square test of relationship has been applied. The Kruskal-Wallis one-way analysis of variance test has also been run on the kinesthetic and sociofugal-sociopetal measures, which serves to strengthen the reliability of the chi-square.[12]

Common measures for degree of association such as Gamma, Kendall's Tau B or Tau C have not been utilized as they also assume ordinality of data. Since the SPSS package was used in processing the data, those test statistics from the package which are amenable to nominal data were employed. One such measure for degree of association available within the crosstabs subroutine is Cramer's V, which is intimately related to the commonly used ϕ and X^2

$$V^2 = \frac{X^2}{N\min(r-1,\ c-1)} = \frac{\phi^2}{\min(r-1,\ c-1)}$$

measures. Since Cramer's V is related to chi-square, V^2 is subject to the influence of sample size. If the samples are large, significance can be established when only a weak relationship exists (see Blalock, 1972 ed., 292 et. sec.). Though the Goodman Kruskal tau would have been the most desirable measure of association, this statistic was not available in any statistical package. Difficulty of computation led the authors to choose the other measures.

Proxemic variable I: Position

Hall   has   defined   this   variable   in   a   manner   which
delineates   at   least   two   distinct   phenomena.   First,   the
measure   divides   by   sex,   and   second,   by   body   position--
whether   a   subject   was   lying   down,   sitting   on   a   chair,   or
standing.   For purposes of this analysis a position has been
inserted between the last two to account for those sitting
on   bar   stools.   The   major   problem   with   these   measures   is
that they are both discrete and arbitrary in nature.   Thus,
one is unsure of how to code an individual who is resting
with his or her posterior on the edge of a table or leaning
with elbows on the bar.   Kinesic recording, which codes much
more   minute   postural   variations   can   account   for   this   lack,
though all codes proposed to date divide the action spectrum
in an analytically arbitrary way (the units bear no speci-
fiable   relation   to   a   code   of   indigenous   cultural   meanings).

At one level of analysis both male and female subjects
have been combined to compare behaviors across groups, but
male,   female,   and   cross-sex   interactions   have   also   been
distinguished at other levels.   A look at the observed cell
frequencies reveals that the Italians utilized chairs the
most   often,   followed   by   the   Mexicans,   Irish,   Serbians,
Americans, and Germans.   Most significant is the fact that
in the Polish bars tables were available, yet the Poles
chose not to utilize them.   Tables were lacking in the Greek
bars eliminating any choices of seating apparatus.

A cursory glance at the contingency table reveals that
most   groups   selected   the   standing   position   about   equally
(15-20% of the time), with the exception of the Greeks and

Germans. Increased incidence of standing in the Greek bar can be accounted for by one situational shift at time three of bar #10; a short span of interaction and lack of stools created this condition (see bar map and contingency table). The standing exhibited by the Germans appears to reflect cultural preference; a point corroborated by Hall's observations (1969: 137). Bar stools were selected most often by the Polish, followed by the Greeks, Irish, Americans, Serbians, and Germans. In some cases this reflects preferences within the ethnic groups. To attribute all such variations to ethnic preference would be erroneous. Though the motivations behind such selections were not questioned by the investigators, in large part this measure is situationally determined. The chi-square value which is significant at the .001 level can be attributed primarily to situational variations rather than to ethnic preference.

In many establishments there were relatively few tables compared with the number of stools; furthermore, the tables were often used for storing groceries and stacking coats. To assume that a person 'y' chose to sit on a stool because such action is normative for a member of group 'Y' overlooks situation-specific factors. On the other hand, to assume that bringing one's groceries into a bar is a situationally meaningful rather than a culturally meaningful act could be in error. The choice to study similar and contrastive settings within each ethnic group was aimed at sorting out such relevant domains for various action schemas.

As would be expected, virtually no variation in position was found within the churches. The only cases which were not recorded as 'standing' occurred in the Italian church where two young boys were observed sitting on a ledge outside of the church. Age and perhaps sex are meaningful identity correlates which qualify the action as

163

acceptable within this setting. The lack of variability among groups in the churches is a result of context, yet it also reflects shared European/American beliefs about appropriate ritual actions. A brief comparison with Pacific Islanders, for example, would show that at least 70% of the latter group would elect to sit in the shade to conduct their after-church conversations. Thus, the lack of variation in our sample does not mean that communicative choices are not being made at the cultural level.

Statistical Results for Position Measure

Using each bar separately:

$x^2 = 312.28760$ df = 36   sig. = .001

cramer's V = .49705

Bars combined:

$x^2 = 182.87785$ df = 7   sig. = .001

cramer's V = .38037

Churches:

$x^2 = 40.88878$ df = 7   sig. = .001

cramer's V = .38490

Ethnic Group	Bar	Time	Measurement Category				
			1 (2)	3 (4)	5 (6)	7 (8)	
MEXICAN	01	1		2	3	1	
		2		8	2		
		3			4	2	
		sum		10	9	3	
	11	1		4	1	3	
		2		6	4		
		3		6	5	3	
		sum		16	10	6	
		tot		26	19	9	54
POLISH	02	1			10		
		2			14		
		3			11	5	
		sum			35	5	
	12	1			13	1	
		2			9	3	
		3			9	1	
		sum			31	5	
		tot			66	10	76
GERMAN	04	1			4		
		3			1	5	
		sum			5	5	
	05	1		6	16	2	
		2		3	8	1	
		3		4	2		
		sum		13	26	3	
	15	1			6	10	
		2			6	6	
		3			5	3	
		sum			17	19	
		tot		13	48	27	88
ITALIAN	06	1		6			
		2		8			
		3			6	2	
		sum		14	6	2	
	16	1		6	4	10	
		2		18		6	
		3		20	4	4	
		sum		44	8	20	
		tot		58	14	22	94

	Bar	Time	1 (2)	3 (4)	5 (6)	7 (8)	
S	07	1		2	2		
E		2		6	2		
R		3		2	4	4	
B		sum		10	8	4	
I	17	1			6	2	
A		2			5	1	
N		3			9	3	
		sum			20	6	
		tot		10	28	10	48
I	08	1			6		
R		2			12		
I		sum			18		
S	13	1		14	12	2	
H		2		14	11	1	
		3		12	8		
		sum		40	31	3	
	18	1			13	1	
		2			11	1	
		3			16	2	
		sum			40	4	
		tot		40	89	7	136
A	09	1		2	11	3	
M		2			5	5	
E		3			7	5	
R		sum		2	23	13	
I	19	1		8	10		
C		2		2	9	1	
A		3		2	8		
N		sum		12	27	1	
		tot		14	50	14	78
G	10	1			7	1	
R		2			8	4	
E		3			11	13	
E		sum			26	18	
K	20	1			3	1	
		2			8		
		3			5	1	
		sum			16	2	
		tot			42	20	62
			0	161	356	115	632

Observed / Expected Frequencies

for Position Measure

ethnic group		1	3	5	7	T=
Mexican	B		26 / 13.8	19 / 30.4	9 / 9.8	54
	C			0 / .8	36 / 35.2	36
	G		26 / 15.9	19 / 35.9	45 / 38.2	90
Polish	B		0 / 19.4	66 / 42.8	10 / 13.8	76
	C			0 / .8	36 / 35.2	36
	G		0 / 19.9	66 / 44.7	46 / 47.5	112
German	B		10 / 22.4	48 / 49.6	27 / 16.0	88
	C			0 / .7	34 / 33.3	34
	G		13 / 21.6	48 / 48.6	61 / 51.7	122
Italian	B		58 / 22.9	14 / 50.7	18 / 16.4	90
	C			6 / .8	30 / 35.2	36
	G		58 / 22.3	20 / 50.2	48 / 53.4	126
Serbian	B		10 / 12.2	28 / 27.0	10 / 8.7	48
	C			0 / .9	40 / 39.1	40
	G		10 / 15.6	28 / 35.1	50 / 37.3	88
Irish	B		40 / 34.6	89 / 76.6	7 / 24.7	136
	C			0 / .7	34 / 33.3	34
	G		40 / 30.1	89 / 67.8	41 / 72.1	170
American	B		14 / 19.9	50 / 43.9	14 / 14.2	78
	C			0 / .8	36 / 35.2	36
	G		14 / 20.2	50 / 45.4	50 / 48.3	114
Greek	B		0 / 15.8	42 / 34.9	20 / 11.3	62
	C			0 / .5	24 / 23.5	24
	G		0 / 15.2	42 / 34.3	44 / 36.5	86
bar totals			161	356	115	632
church totals				6	270	276
group totals			161	362	385	908

B = bar   C = church   G = total group

168

Proxemic variable II: Sociofugal-sociopetal axis

This variable measures the body axis of two individuals involved in a dyadic interaction or a larger 'with'--"0" = direct, front-to-front, through "8" = back-to-back. Since conversational dyads were being observed it was rare to record a score of over "4". Considerable differences among ethnic groups are apparent in the bar setting as evidenced by the chi-square value which is significant at the .001 level. The greatest percentage of front-to-front interactions occurred among the Mexicans, followed by the Serbians and Italians. A look at the observed versus expected frequencies on the contingency table and the associated graphs indicates that nearly all interactions (78% in the Mexican group) fall into the "0" or "1" categories. The Italians and Serbians manifest a more gradual movement toward the less direct categories. In part this reflects situational variations such as the greater number of "2's" in the Italian bar #16, where one large group of persons was concentrated around a small square table.

The charts indicate that the Germans exhibited the widest range of shoulder axes in the bars; next in line would be Serbians, Italians and Irish in no specific order. The most restricted range was observed in the Greek bars where the shoulder axes never assumed more than a 120 degree angle (coded "3"). This might be a matter of ethnic choice combined with the tendency to maintain direct eye contact along with direct shoulder axes (the Greeks and Italians maintain the highest degree of eye contact). The Americans tended to utilize the most balanced range of shoulder axes,

never exceeding 30% or dipping below 10% in the categories
they employed. The Polish tended to be the most indirect,
relying on the "3" and "4" axes most often, though never
exceeding a "4". The ranks based upon the Kruskal-Wallis
test order the bar groups in the following manner: Mexican,
Italian, Serbian, Greek, American, Irish and German
(virtually equivalent rankings), and Polish. As previously
noted, this shows the Mexicans to be the most 'direct' and
the Polish to be the least 'direct' in shoulder axis
configuration.

In the churches the range of shoulder axes proved to be
more restricted than was the case in the barroom setting.
The tables indicate that in the bars the axes utilized range
from "0" to "6", while in the churches the range varies from
"0" to "4". Although the differences in the ranges between
these settings appear striking, this impression is somewhat
deceptive. The occurrences of "5s" and "6s" are actually
quite rare even in the bars. With regard to all bars
considered, only in twelve cases was the score of "5"
recorded, and only two "6s" were noted in the 632 total
observations. Of course, we have restricted our measures to
interacting 'withs', and back-to-back positions generally
signify non-interaction. '5s' and '6s' allow a person to
split themselves into two marginally-attentive beings and
play both roles simultaneously. Thus, one may play the role
of listener in a television drama and still attend to a
second 'live' performance (as in Italian bar #6). Had we
chosen to record non-interactions, we would have had many
'6s' '7s' and '8s' in our records for non-interacting people
in the identical setting. At the same time, however, many
'0s' and '1s' would be recorded for people who were not
communicating with one another--chance face-to-face shoulder
configurations among non-interacting persons (person 8 and
person 9 in Mexican bar #11 [time 1] are one such example).

170

Of course, face-to-face configurations set up the conditions for communication between non-interacting occupants of the same physical space, but they do not guarantee that any messages will be sent or received. For example, two members of different 'withs' seated at adjacent booths or tables and facing one another may exchange glances and smiles, creating a new 'with'. But the configuration does not require any information to change hands. On this account we constructed our records by attending to interacting 'withs' at each recording time.

One might hypothesize that in an environment such as a church's entryway, where there is little obstruction in terms of semi-fixed spatial configurations (such as furniture in the bars), any preference along the sociofugal-sociopetal scale by any ethnic group would be particularly evident. In this uncluttered setting the Serbians, Germans, and Polish show a preference for the face-to-face position. The Irish did not employ this axis but show a strong preference for "1's". The Americans show the strongest preference for sociofugal-sociopetal axis "3", with more than 44% of the interactions occurring in this configuration, while only 5.6% occur at axis "0". The Greeks in this sample also exhibit a preference for sociofugal-sociopetal axis "3". The Mexicans have an equal preference for "1's" and "3's". The chi-square test indicates that the differences among the ethnic churches are significant at the .01 level. The Kruskal-Wallis test confirms that the church rankings are significantly different from the bar rankings. This lack of systematic correspondence indicates great situational variation within ethnic groups. The church rankings, most direct listed first, are as follows: Serbian, Polish, Italian, German, Mexican, Greek, Irish, and American. The lack of situational homogeneity is indicated by the combined (bar plus church) Kruskal-Wallis test.

These ranks are almost totally controlled by the much larger sample of bars (sample sizes: 632 vs. 276), yielding the skewed lumped group rankings of: Mexican, Serbian, Italian, Greek, German, American, Polish, and Irish.

Hall (1963, 1009) asserts that, "0, 1, 2, 4, and 8 are most frequently observed." The data gathered in this study clearly indicates a different pattern. In the structured environment of the bar "3", "2", "0", "1", "4", "5", and "6" occur in that order of frequency. In the church setting the order is "3", "1", "2", "0", and "4". In the lumped sample the most frequent configuration is the "3", occurring in 350 of the 908 cases, that is, in 175 of the 454 dyadic interactions observed. The versatility of this axis may account for its predominance in that it allows an interactant to engage his or her counterpart without ruling out one's openness to the surrounding milieu. Hall's comment that "8's" should be frequently observed seems absurd. Indeed, Chic Young's use of this configuration in the comic strip 'Blondie' serves as a classical comical device (it indexes the refusal of Dagwood and Blondie to carry on a meaningful conversation).

Some problems were encountered in coding this variable. For instance, a "4" would necessarily be recorded if two persons were standing shoulder to shoulder or back to front, two interaction patterns which might connote very different things. Likewise, a position might be observed which was left shoulder to left shoulder (or right to right), yet using Hall's coding schema it needs be recorded as a "0" or an "8", neither adequately expressing the actual situation (see diagram on following page). In correlating the visual, distance, and axis measures, it appears that at a greater distance individuals in interaction tend to have more direct axis and exhibit more direct eye contact. The authors have

172

no statistical support for this data-inspired hypothesis.

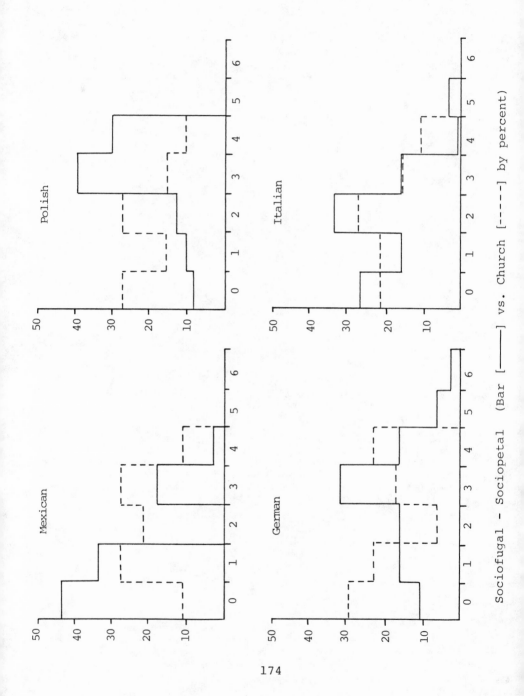

Sociofugal - Sociopetal   (Bar [———] vs. Church [-----] by percent)

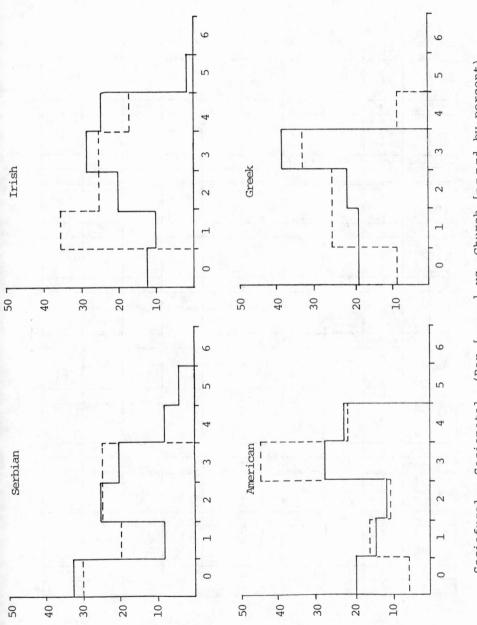

Sociofugal - Sociopetal (Bar [————] vs. Church [- - - -] by percent)

Sociofugal - Sociopetal

Ethnic Group	Bar	Time	0	1	2	3	4	5	6	7	8	
MEXICAN	01	1	2			4						
		2	8			2						
		3	4				2					
		sum	14			6	2					
	11	1	4	4								
		2	2	6		2						
		3	4	8		2						
		sum	10	18		4						
		tot	24	18		10	2					54
POLISH	02	1				4	6					
		2				6	8					
		3		4	2	8	2					
		sum		4	2	18	16					
	12	1			6	4	4					
		2	2	4	2	4	4					
		3	4			4	2					
		sum	6	4	8	12	6					
		tot	6	8	10	30	22					76
GERMAN	04	1	2				2	2				
		2		2		2						
		sum	2	2		2	2	2				
	05	1	2	4	4	8	6					
		2	2		4	4		2				
		3	2			2	2					
		sum	6	4	8	14	8	2				
	15	1	2	2	2	8	2					
		2		4	2	4			2			
		3		2	2		2	2				
		sum	2	8	6	12	4	2	2			
		tot	10	14	14	28	14	6	2			88
ITALIAN	06	1	4	2								
		2	2	2	2			2				
		3	2	2		2	2					
		sum	8	6	2	2	2	2				
	16	1	4	4	6	6						
		2	6	4	10	4						
		3	6	4	10	4						
		sum	16	12	26	14						
		tot	24	18	28	16	2	2				90

Sociofugal - Sociopetal (continued)

	Bar	Time	0	1	2	3	4	5	6	7	8	
S E R B I A N	07	1	2			2						
		2	4				2	2				
		3	4		4		2					
		sum	10		4	2	4	2				
	17	1	2	2	2	2						
		2	2		2	2						
		3	2	2	4	4						
		sum	6	4	8	8						
		tot	16	4	12	10	4	2				48
I R I S H	08	1				6						
		2		6	4		2					
		sum		6	4	6	2					
	13	1	6	2	8	4	6	2				
		2	2	4	6	8	6					
		3	2	2	6	4	6					
		sum	10	8	20	16	18	2				
	18	1	2		2	8	4					
		2	2			4	6					
		3	4		4	6	4					
		sum	8		6	18	14					
		tot	18	14	30	40	34	2				136
A M E R I C A N	09	1	2	2		4	8					
		2	4	2		2	2					
		3	6	4		2						
		sum	12	8		8	10					
	19	1	4		4	6	4					
		2		4	2	2	4					
		3			4	6						
		sum	4	4	10	14	8					
		tot	16	12	10	22	18					78
G R E E K	10	1	2	4	2							
		2	2	4	6							
		3		4	6	14						
		sum	4	12	14	14						
	20	1	4									
		2	2			6						
		3	2			4						
		sum	8			10						
		tot	12	12	14	24						62
			126	98	118	180	96	12	2			632

Statistical Results for Sociofugal - Sociopetal Measure

Using each bar separately:

x^2 = 353.31348   df = 102   sig. = .001

cramer's V = .30524

Bars combined:

x^2 = 168.91319   df = 42   sig. = .001

cramer's V = .21106

Churches:

x^2 = 52.06683   df = 28   sig. = .01

Observed / Expected Frequencies

for Sociofugal - Sociopetal Measure

ethnic group		0	1	2	3	4	5	6	7	8	T=
Mexican	B	24/10.8	18/8.4	0/10.1	10/15.3	2/8.2	0/1.1	0/.2			54
	C	4/6.3	10/8.3	8/7.6	10/9.1	4/4.7					36
	G	28/17.2	28/16.1	8/17.4	20/24.8	6/13.1	0/1.2	0/.2			90
Polish	B	6/15.2	8/11.8	10/14.2	30/21.5	22/11.5	0/1.6	0/.2			76
	C	10/6.3	6/8.3	10/7.6	6/9.1	4/4.7					36
	G	16/21.5	14/20.0	20/21.7	36/30.8	26/16.3	0/1.5	0/.2			112
German	B	10/17.5	14/13.6	14/16.4	28/24.9	14/13.4	6/1.8	2/.3			88
	C	10/5.9	8/7.9	2/7.1	6/8.6	8/4.4					34
	G	20/23.4	22/21.8	16/23.6	34/33.6	22/17.7	6/1.6	2/.3			122
Italian	B	24/17.9	16/13.9	30/16.8	16/25.5	2/13.7	2/1.9	0/.3			90
	C	8/6.3	8/8.3	10/7.6	6/9.1	4/4.7					36
	G	32/24.1	24/22.5	40/24.4	22/34.7	6/18.3	2/1.7	0/.3			126
Serbian	B	16/9.6	4/7.4	12/8.9	10/13.6	4/7.3	2/1.0	0/.2			48
	C	12/7.0	8/9.3	10/8.4	10/10.1	0/5.2					40
	G	28/16.9	12/15.7	22/17.1	20/24.2	4/12.8	2/1.2	0/.2			88
Irish	B	18/27.1	14/21.1	28/25.3	40/38.5	34/20.7	2/2.8	0/.4			136
	C	0/5.9	12/7.9	8/7.1	8/8.6	6/4.4					34
	G	18/32.6	26/30.3	36/33.0	48/46.8	40/24.7	2/2.2	0/.4			170
American	B	16/15.6	12/12.1	10/14.6	22/22.1	18/11.8	0/1.6	0/.2			78
	C	2/6.3	6/8.3	4/7.6	16/9.1	8/4.7					36
	G	18/6.9	18/20.3	14/22.1	38/31.4	26/16.6	0/1.5	0/.3			114
Greek	B	12/12.4	12/9.6	14/17.2	24/17.6	0/9.4	0/1.3	0/.2			62
	C	2/4.2	6/5.6	6/5.0	8/6.1	2/3.1					24
	G	14/16.5	18/15.3	20/16.7	32/23.7	2/12.5	0/1.1	0/.2			86
bar totals		126	98	118	180	96	12	2			632
church totals		48	64	58	70	36					276
group totals		174	162	176	250	132	12	2			908

B = bar   C = church   G = total group

Kruskal-Wallis One-Way Analysis of Variance

Sample = Bar   Measure = sociofugal/sociopetal

Ethnic Group

Mex.	Pol.	Ger.	Ital.	Serb.	Irish	Amer.	Greek	Rank	Measure	Total
24	6	10	24	16	18	16	12	63.5	0	126
18	8	14	16	4	14	12	12	175.5	1	98
	10	14	30	12	28	10	14	283.5	2	118
10	30	28	16	10	40	22	24	432.5	3	180
2	22	14	2	4	34	18		569.5	4	96
		6	2	2	2			624.5	5	12
		2						631.5	6	2
54	76	88	90	48	136	78	62			632

10142	30109	32137	22191	12996	49566	25712	17205	= sum R_i's

187.8148	396.1710	365.1931	246.5611	270.1250	364.4595	329.6410	277.5000	= $\bar{R}_i$

616.3935	437.9638	378.2414	369.8361	693.4427	244.7444	426.7339	536.8588	= $\dfrac{(N^2-1)}{12n_i}$

26.8679	6.3342	6.2677	13.2262	3.1007	9.3983	.4046	2.8331	= $\dfrac{(\bar{R} - [N+1]/2)^2}{([N^2-1]/12n_i}$

sum of above = 68.4327

$\dfrac{N-1}{N}$ = .9984

.9984 x 68.4327 = 68.3232

$\dfrac{68.3232}{.956}$ = 71.467 with df=7

sig. =.001

180

Kruskal-Wallis One Way Analysis of Variance

Sample = Church   **Measure = Sociofugal/Sociopetal**

Ethnic Group

Mex.	Pol.	Ger.	Ital.	Serb.	Irish	Amer.	Greek	Rank	Measure	Total
4	10	10	8	12		2	2	24.5	0	48
10	6	8	8	8	12	6	6	80.5	1	64
8	10	2	10	10	8	4	6	141.5	2	58
10	6	6	6	10	8	16	8	205.5	3	70
4	4	8	4		6	8	2	258.5	4	36
36	36	34	36	40	34	36	24			276

5124	4410	4473	4522	4408	5293	6454	3542	= sum R_i's

142.3333	122.5000	131.5588	125.6111	110.2000	155.6764	179.2777	147.5833	= $\bar{R}_i$

176.3310	176.3310	186.7034	174.7133	158.6979	186.7034	176.3310	264.4964	= $\dfrac{(N^2-1)}{12n_i}$

.0831	1.4518	.2579	.9510	5.0465	1.5808	9.4312	.3117	= $\dfrac{(\bar{R} - [N+1]/2)^2}{([N^2-1]/12n_i)}$

sum of above = 19.1140

$\dfrac{N-1}{N}$ = .9963   .9963 x 19.1140 = 19.0432

.955 = correction for ties

$\dfrac{19.0432}{.955}$ = 19.940 with df=7

sig. = .01

181

Kruskal-Wallis One-Way Analysis of Variance

Sample = Bars + Churches (Combined)

Measure = sociofugal/sociopetal

<u>Ethnic Group</u>

Mex.	Pol.	Ger.	Ital.	Serb.	Irish	Amer.	Greek	Rank	Measure	Total
28	16	20	32	28	18	18	14	87.5	0	174
28	14	22	24	12	26	18	18	255.5	1	162
8	20	16	40	22	36	14	20	424.5	2	176
20	36	34	22	20	48	38	32	637.5	3	250
6	26	22	6	4	40	26	2	827.5	4	132
		6	2	2	2			899.5	5	12
		2						907.5	6	2
90	112	122	126	88	170	114	86			908

	Pol.		Ger.		Serb.		Amer.	
	57914		46764		89166		36353	
Mex. 19239		Ital. 61241		21239		Irish 57838		= sum of R_i's

Mex.	Pol.	Ger.	Ital.	Serb.	Irish	Amer.	Greek	
213.7666	517.0892	501.9754	371.1388	241.3522	524.5088	507.3508	422.7093	$= \bar{R}_i$
763.3916	613.4397	563.1577	545.2797	780.7414	404.1485	602.6776	798.8982	$= \dfrac{(N^2-1)}{12n_i}$
75.9126	6.3698	4.0030	12.7437	58.1921	12.1276	4.6345	1.2649	$= \dfrac{(\bar{R}-[N+1]/2)^2}{([N^2-1]/12n_i)}$

sum of above = 175.2482

$\dfrac{N-1}{N}$ = .9988   .9988 x 175.2482 = 175.0379

.957 = correction for ties $\dfrac{175.0379}{.957}$ = 182.901 with df=7

sig. = .001

Proxemic variable III: Kinesthetic

This variable is likely that which best characterizes
folk conceptions of proxemics -- it measures the distance
which individuals keep between themselves and others, their
"personal" space which, if invaded without permission, forms
a virtual offense requiring a "remedial interchange" (in
Goffman's terms). Hall, though, has quite a different view
of what his kinesthetic code is able to record. He claims
that:

> Since two parties are involved and each has his
> own repertoire of the 8 kinesthethic distances used,
> it is possible to construct a matrix with eight
> dimensions on a side (one for each kinesthetic
> distance) which contains 64 slots (8 x 8). Because
> such a matrix is nothing more than a mechanical way of
> insuring that all possible combinations have been
> accounted for, there is considerable duplication (13
> and 31 for example).

Hall's argument assumes that the analytic units are cultural
units carried around unconsciously in the minds of actors.
Yet no evidence is offered that indicates that either party
to an interaction has a "repertoire of the 8 kinesthetic
distances".   If the units did reflect such cultural
boundaries the problem would then be shifted to Hall's
matrix analysis. Interpersonal spacing, as indicated by the
term itself, is a conception which is inherently mediated
and dyadic. The distances between two interactants can only

be defined relationally, vis-à-vis one another. The kinesthetic distance of one interactant cannot be separated from that of the co-interactant. Yet, a matrix that plots combinations of individual spatial configurations assumes that interpersonal space can be divided in this way. It rejects a mediated view of interaction in favor of an atomistic one. If one takes seriously such an individualized view of human action, the matrix model is applicable without any duplication. Thus, a spatial coding of "1" for individual "a" and "3" for individual "b", as implied by a "13" on the matrix would be very different from a "3" for individual "a" and a "1" for individual "b". The intended meanings would be quite distinct since, in each example, "a" and "b" selected different, non-symetrical, spatial configurations.

The fallacy in Hall's approach derives from the fact that individuals do not carry around with them closed spatial spheres to protect them from invasion. Interpersonal space is not divisible into personal space "a" plus personal space "b" which can then be plotted on a matrix.

	1	10	2	20	3	30	. . .
1	11	110	12	120	13	130	
10	101	1010	102	1020	103	1030	
2	21	210	22	220	23	230	
20	201	2010	202	2020	203	2030	
3	31	310	32	320	33	330	
30	301	3010	302	3020	303	3030	
.							
.	(Portion of Hall's Matrix -- i., j. distribution)
.							

Interpersonal space is a mediated concept which is constituted relationally. In Durkheimian terms, it is sui

184

<u>generis</u> a social fact.   Therefore, we have redefined Hall's
atomistic scale (1963: 1010) so it is suited to record
dyadic interactions (see definition of measures).

   The results of the chi-square and the Kruskal-Wallis
tests on the kinesthetic data are significant at the .001
level which indicate a number of differences among ethnic
groups.   The raw frequencies and the within-group percentages show that the groups that space themselves most
closely in the bar setting are the Mexican, Greek, and
Italian, in that order.   The German sample exhibits the
widest range of action.   The German pattern also closely
resembles the pattern of the American sample.   This is not
unexpected in that the Germans represent a long-standing
Chicago ethnic group, once of considerable size but today
dispersed throughout various quadrants of the city.   The
American sample was not chosen to be totally representative.
It was selected to derive some normative patterns for the
'middle-class', a group much discussed by Hall and
Birdwhistell in rather vague terms.   We based our sample
"American community ' on Chicago residents' notions of what
they considered representative of a "typical middle class
community."   The second American bar, #19, best approximated
the authors' conceptions of this ideal while bar #9 was less
successful at maintaining the same facade.

   The Irish spaced themselves farthest from each other,
as did the Polish group who exhibited the most balanced
range of action.   Within the two bars of this latter group
some extreme differences can be seen.   In large part this
reflects spatial relations structured by the seating pattern
at the bar (see map and network on following pages).   In the
second Polish bar the interactions taking place across the
bar have a dramatic effect on the kinesthetic scores, as do
the crowded conditions in the first Polish bar.   The closest

185

distance observed in the first Polish bar is a "10", while
in the second the closest interaction distance is a "20", a
shift of two categories. In spite of greater interaction
distances in the second bar, the touch scores on the lower
end of the scale (spot touching and holding), do not differ
notably. The Serbians in the sample, whose intra-bar differences mainly reflect extreme variation in the interaction
styles of the bartenders, serve as an example intermediate
between the Irish-Polish group and the German case. The
Kruskal-Wallis test gives a ranking of: Greek, Mexican,
Italian, German, Serbian, Polish, Irish, and American.
These results indicate that the Americans space themselves
farthest apart. A look at the raw data for the American
sample reveals that the first three interaction categories
are almost entirely void. The preponderance of interactions
over "30" largely can be attributed to the bartender's long-
distance style of interaction with the customers and barmaids.

The church rankings are, with some exception, quite
similar to the kinesthetic orderings in the bars: Greek,
Serbian, Italian, Mexican and Polish (equivalent rankings),
American, and German. Both the Mexican and German samples
represented more highly acculturated groups than the corresponding bar samples. This may help to explain the shift
toward the more distant interaction style of the American
middle class church. Inspection of the church data reveals
that the Greeks exhibit the only instances of "1s" on the
kinesthetic code, with 16% of their interactions falling in
this category. There are two anomalous "5s" among the Greek
group, occasioned by the swing-pattern of the doors leading
from the church. To avoid being hit by the doors the dyad
in question was forced to stand at a distance which allowed
no possible contact (coded as a "5" on the kinesthetic
scale). This is an aberrant case, since there are no

instances of interaction in the four intervening cells (03, 30, 04, 40). All other interactions among the Greeks took place at close range -- from "1" to "20". Other narrow ranges were displayed by the Serbians and Italians. These groups show a definite preference for close distances, with the range extending from "10" to "3". Most of the other groups span five distance categories. The Germans, however, span seven distance categories and show a preference for the interaction distance of "30" (29% of the Germans sampled use this distance as compared with 9.4% of the total sample). As noted, this wide range of actions among the Germans was also observed in the bars.

The Irish do not utilize distances "1" and "10" but show a preference to interact at a distance recorded as a "20" (29.4% of the observations were at this distance). The Americans, the Irish, and the Germans are the most balanced, though the first two groups exhibit a narrower range of preferred interaction distances.

Sommer (1967, 149) comments: "The idea that Females can tolerate closer physical presence than males is underscored by observations of women holding hands or kissing one another, practices which are uncommon between males in this culture." Sommer seems unsure of the weight to be given to innate tendency and cultural influences in her statement, and we certainly have no evidence that close physical proximity is any more a matter of toleration than it is of cultural choice. Utilizing same-sex interactions, and data from the kinesthetic code, we can say that the Indo-European groups we studied generally support her contention. In no instances within the churches do males utilize the interaction distance of "1", while only the Greek women use this distance. Out of the eight samples, females prefer closer distances in the Greek, Italian,

Serbian, and Polish groups, in that order. The church sample indicates that German and American men prefer closer interaction distances than do the women of these groups. Thus, while Sommer's observation may have some merit, it cannot be extended cross-culturally without regard to the specific group and interactional context in question. While the sample is small and the results are only relevant to specific situations, this study does indicate some typical action scenarios used to express ethnic and gender identities.

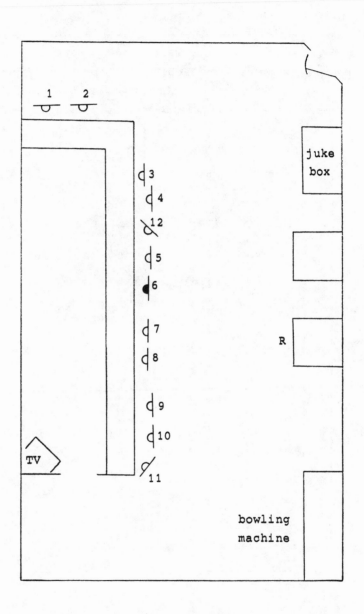

POLISH BAR #2   time 2

189

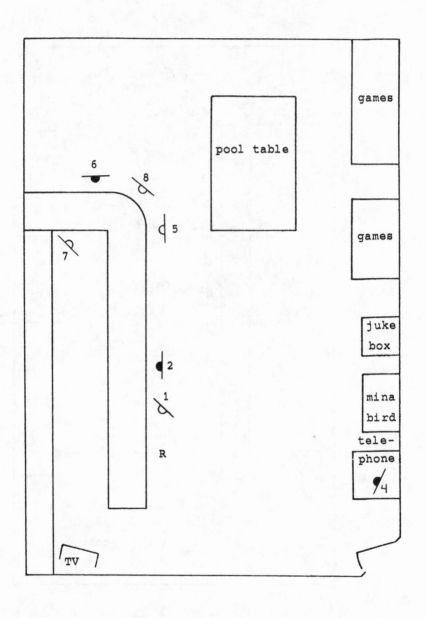

POLISH   BAR   #12   time 2

190

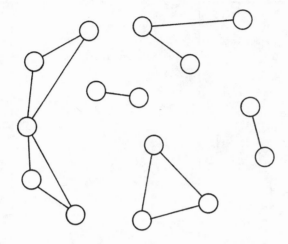

Polish Bar #2

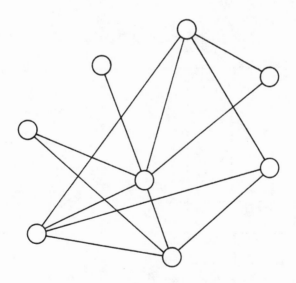

Polish Bar #12

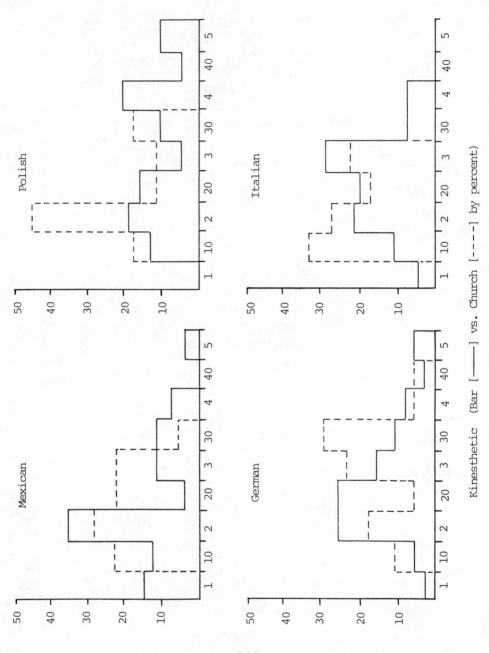

Kinesthetic (Bar [———] vs. Church [- - - -] by percent)

192

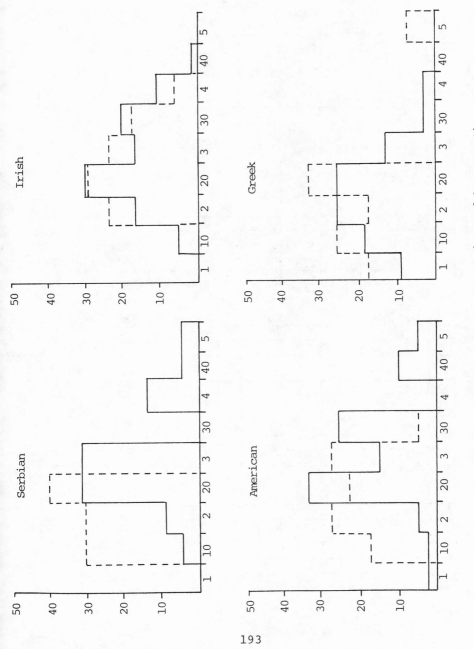

Kinesthetic   (Bar [————] vs. Church [- - - -] by percent)

Kinesthetic

Ethnic Group	Bar	Time	01	10	02	20	03	30	04	40	05	
MEXICAN	01	1			2		2	2				
		2	2		6		2					
		3	2	2	2							
		sum	4	2	10		4	2				
	10	1			2			4			2	
		2	2	2	2		2		2			
		3	2	4	4	2			2			
		sum	4	6	8	2	2	4	4		2	
		tot	8	8	18	2	6	6	4		2	54
POLISH	02	1		4	4		2					
		2		4	4	2		2	2			
		3		2	6			2	6			
		sum		10	14	2	2	4	8			
	12	1				4		2	2	2	4	
		2				2	2		2	2		
		3				4		2			4	
		sum				10	2	4	4	4	8	
		tot		10	14	12	4	8	12	4	8	72
GERMAN	04	1			2	2						
		3	2	2							2	
		sum	2	2	2	2					2	
	05	1			6	4	4	6	2		2	
		2			6	2	4					
		3		2	2		2					
		sum		2	14	6	10	6	2		2	
	15	1			2	8	2	2		2		
		2			2	4		2	4			
		3			2	2	2		2			
		sum			6	14	4	4	6	2		
		tot	2	4	22	22	14	10	8	2	4	88
ITALIAN	06	1			4	2						
		2			4	4						
		3		4			4					
		sum		4	8	6	4					
	16	1	2	6	2		6	4				
		2	2		4	6	8	2	2			
		3			6	6	8		4			
		sum	4	6	12	12	22	6	6			
		tot	4	10	20	18	26	6	6			90

194

	Bar	Time	01	10	02	20	03	30	04	40	05	
S E R B I A N	07	1				2	2					
		2			2	2	4					
		3		2		6	2					
		sum		2	2	10	8					
	17	1				4			4			
		2			2		4					
		3				2	4		2	2	2	
		sum			2	6	8		6	2	2	
		tot		2	4	16	16		6	2	2	48
I R I S H	08	1	4			2						
		2	2			4	6					
		sum	6			6	6					
	13	1			6	8	6	8				
		2			6	6	6	6	2			
		3			4	6	4	4	2			
		sum			16	20	16	18	4			
	18	1			6			4	2	2		
		2				6		2	4			
		3				8	2	4	4			
		sum			6	14	2	10	10	2		
		tot		6	22	40	24	28	14	2		136
A M E R I C A N	09	1				4	4	8				
		2	2			4		2			2	
		3				4		4		2	2	
		sum	2			12	4	14		2	4	
	19	1			2	8	2	6				
		2		2		2	4			4		
		3			2	4	2			2		
		sum		2	4	14	8	6		6		
		tot	2	2	4	26	12	20		8	4	78
G R E E K	10	1			2	2	2	2				
		2			2	6	2		2			
		3	4	10	6	4						
		sum	4	10	10	12	4	2	2			
	20	1			2	2						
		2			2	2	4					
		3	2	2	2							
		sum	2	2	6	4	4					
		tot	6	12	16	16	8	2	2			62
			22	53	121	153	109	80	56	18	20	632

195

Statistical Results for Kinesthetic Measure

Using each bar separately:

x^2 = 457.94263   df = 136   sig. = .001

cramer's V = .30096

Bars combined:

x^2 = 223.40286   df = 56   sig. = .001

cramer's V = .22472

Churches:

x^2 = 170.88556   df = 56   sig. = .001

cramer's V = .29741

Observed / Expected Frequencies

for Kinesthetic Measure

ethnic group		01	10	02	20	03	30	04	40	05	T=
Mexican	B	8/1.9	8/4.5	18/10.3	2/13.1	6/9.3	6/9.1	4/4.8	0/1.5	2/1.7	54
	C	0/.5	8/7.0	10/9.9	8/8.1	8/6.0	2/3.4	0/.5	0/.3	0/.3	36
	G	8/2.5	16/10.6	28/19.5	10/21.3	14/15.4	8/10.5	4/5.9	0/1.8	2/2.0	90
Polish	B	0/2.6	10/6.4	14/14.6	12/18.4	4/13.1	8/9.6	16/6.7	4/2.2	8/2.4	76
	C	0/.5	6/7.0	16/9.9	4/8.1	4/6.0	6/3.4	0/.5	0/.3	0/.3	36
	G	0/3.2	16/13.2	30/24.3	16/26.5	8/19.1	14/13.1	16/7.4	4/2.5	8/2.7	112
German	B	2/3.1	4/7.4	22/16.8	22/21.3	4/15.2	10/11.1	8/7.8	2/7.8	4/2.8	88
	C	0/.5	4/6.7	6/9.4	2/7.6	8/5.7	10/3.2	2/.5	2/.2	0/.2	34
	G	2/3.5	8/14.4	28/26.5	24/28.9	22/20.8	20/14.2	10/8.1	4/2.7	4/3.0	122
Italian	B	4/3.1	10/7.5	20/17.2	18/21.8	26/15.5	6/11.4	6/8.0	0/2.6	0/2.8	90
	C	0/.5	12/7.0	10/9.9	6/8.1	8/6.0	0/3.4	0/.5	0/.3	0/.3	36
	G	4/3.6	22/14.8	30/27.3	24/29.8	34/21.5	6/14.7	6/8.3	0/2.8	0/3.1	126
Serbian	B	0/1.7	2/4.0	4/9.2	16/11.6	16/8.3	0/6.1	6/4.3	2/1.4	2/1.5	48
	C	0/.6	12/7.8	12/11.0	16/9.0	0/6.7	0/3.8	0/.6	0/.3	0/.3	40
	G	0/2.5	14/10.4	16/19.1	32/20.8	16/15.0	0/10.3	6/5.8	2/1.9	2/2.1	88
Irish	B	0/4.7	6/11.4	22/26.0	42/32.9	22/23.5	28/17.2	14/12.1	0/3.9	0/4.3	136
	C	0/.5	0/6.7	8/9.4	10/7.6	8/5.7	6/3.2	2/.5	0/.2	0/.2	34
	G	0/4.9	6/20.0	30/36.9	52/40.3	30/29.0	34/19.8	16/11.2	2/3.7	0/3.7	170
American	B	2/2.7	2/6.5	4/14.9	26/18.9	12/13.5	20/9.9	0/6.9	8/2.2	4/2.5	78
	C	0/.5	6/7.0	10/9.9	8/8.1	10/6.0	2/3.4	0/.5	0/.3	0/.3	36
	G	2/3.3	8/13.4	14/24.7	34/27.0	22/19.5	22/13.3	0/7.5	8/2.5	4/2.8	114
Greek	B	6/2.2	12/5.2	16/11.9	16/15.0	8/10.7	2/7.8	2/5.5	0/1.8	0/2.0	62
	C	4/.3	6/4.7	4/6.6	8/5.4	0/4.0	0/2.3	0/.3	0/.2	2/.2	24
	G	10/2.5	18/10.1	20/18.7	24/20.4	8/14.7	2/10.0	2/5.7	0/1.9	2/2.1	86
bar totals		22	54	120	154	108	80	56	18	20	632
church totals		·4	54	76	62	46	26	4	2	2	276
group totals		26	108	196	216	154	106	60	20	22	908

B = bar   C = church   G = total group

Kruskal-Wallis One-Way Analysis of Variance

Sample = Bar Measure = kinesthetic

Ethnic Group

Mex.	Pol.	Ger.	Ital.	Serb.	Irish	Amer.	Greek	Rank	Measure	Total
8		2	4			2	6	11.5	1	22
8	10	4	10	2	6	2	12	49.5	10	54
18	14	22	20	4	22	4	16	135.5	2	120
2	12	22	18	16	42	26	16	373.5	20	154
6	4	14	26	16	22	12	8	403.5	3	108
6	8	10	6		28	20	2	498.5	30	80
4	16	8	6	6	14		2	566.5	4	56
	4	2		2	2	8		603.5	40	18
2	8	4				4		622.5	5	20
54	76	88	90	48	136	78	62			632

Mex.	Pol.	Ger.	Ital.	Serb.	Irish	Amer.	Greek	
12688	28928	31282	26861	17681	51953	32489	14162	= sum of R_i's
234.9629	380.6315	355.4772	298.4555	368.3541	382.0073	416.5256	228.4193	= $\bar{R}_i$
616.3935	437.9638	378.2414	369.8361	693.4427	244.7444	426.7339	536.8588	= $\dfrac{(N^2-1)}{12n_i}$
10.79	9.3904	4.0171	.8799	3.8769	17.5351	23.4480	14.4508	= $\dfrac{(\bar{R} - [N+1]/2)^2}{([N^2-1]/12n_i)}$

sum of above = 84.3882

$\dfrac{N-1}{N} = .9984$ $.9984 \times 84.3882 = 84.2531$

.971 = correction for ties $\dfrac{84.2531}{.971} = 86.769$ with df=7

sig. = .001

198

Krusakal-Wallis One-Way Analysis of Variance

Sample = Church   **Measure = kinesthetic**

Ethnic Group

Mex.	Pol.	Ger.	Ital.	Serb.	Irish	Amer.	Greek	Rank	Measure	Total
							4	2.5	1	4
8	6	4	12	12		6	6	31.5	10	54
10	16	6	10	12	8	10	4	96.5	2	76
8	4	2	6	16	10	8	8	165.5	20	62
8	4	8	8		8	10		219.5	3	46
2	6	10			6	2		255.5	30	26
		2		2				270.5	4	4
		2						273.5	40	2
							2	275.5	5	2
36	36	34	36	40	34	36	24			276
4808	4806	6435	4092	4184	6257	5184	2460	= sum of R_i's		
133.5555	133.5000	189.2647	113.6666	104.6000	184.0294	144.0000	102.5000	= $\bar{R}_i$		
176.3310	176.3310	186.7034	174.7133	158.6979	186.7034	176.3310	264.4965	= $\dfrac{(N^2-1)}{12n_i}$		
.1383	.1417	13.8006	3.5288	7.2413	11.1032	.1715	4.8998	= $\dfrac{(\bar{R}-[N+1]/2)^2}{([N^2-1]/12n_i}$		

sum of above = 41.0252

$\dfrac{N-1}{N}$ = .9963   .9963 x 41.0252 = 40.8734

.955 = correction for ties $\dfrac{40.8734}{.955}$ = 42.798 with df=7

sig. = .001

Kruskal-Wallis One-Way Analysis of Variance

Sample = Bars + Churches   Measure = Kinesthetic

Ethnic Group

Mex.	Pol.	Ger.	Ital.	Serb.	Irish	Amer.	Greek	Rank	Measure	Total
8		2	4			2	10	13.5	1	26
16	16	8	22	14	6	8	18	80.5	10	108
28	30	28	30	16	30	14	20	231.5	2	196
10	16	24	24	32	52	34	24	438.5	20	216
14	8	22	34	16	30	22	8	622.5	3	154
8	14	20	6		34	22	2	753.5	30	106
4	16	10	6	6	16		2	836.5	4	60
	4	4	2	2	2	8		876.5	40	20
2	8	4		2		4	2	897.5	5	22
90	112	122	126	88	170	114	86			908

Mex.	Pol.	Ger.	Ital.	Serb.	Irish	Amer.	Greek	
32307	54851	61912	50008	37383	89847	59692	26686	= sum of R_i's
358.9666	489.7410	507.4754	396.8888	424.8068	528.5117	523.6140	310.3023	= $\bar{R}_i$
763.3916	613.4397	563.1577	545.2797	780.7414	404.1485	602.6776	798.8982	= $\dfrac{(N^2-1)}{12 n_i}$
11.9545	2.0244	4.9841	6.0866	1.1290	13.5530	7.9249	26.0278	= $\dfrac{(\bar{R} -[N+1]/2)^2}{([N^2-1]/12 n_i)}$

$$\frac{N-1}{N} = .9988$$

.968 = correction for ties

sum of above = 73.6843

.9988 x 73.6843 = 73.5958

$$\frac{73.5958}{.968} = 76.027 \text{ with df=7}$$

sig. = .001

Proxemic variable IV: Touch

As used in this study the touch variable records the amount of touching occurring between persons in the various settings.   Hall (1963, 1011), also discusses this measure in terms of the amount of touching, but the categorical criteria he has selected encompass various types of touching as well as amount.   Thus, a scale of discrete cultural categories (touching, holding, and caressing) is interlaced with a continuous analytic criteria based upon amount or degree of involvement.   The researchers eliminated Hall's lower divisions ('feeling or caressing' vs. 'caressing and holding') due to their subjective mode of measurement.   The remaining categories deserve further refinement on the basis of specific cultural criteria.   Various amounts of touching, as well as the boundaries between categories, almost certainly vary from one ethnic group to another.   Thus, what Greeks may consider to be expressed by a category glossed 'spot touching', might for German interactants be considered 'intensive holding'.   For purposes of this study the categories have been utilized in a purely analytic manner.

The touch code serves as a microscopic refinement of the lower end of the kinesthetic code.   The touch code operates as a 'marked case' of the kinesthetic code serving to inform participants in various situations of a standing relationship between the concerned interactants.   The role relations, "we're married', "we're lovers", "we're related",

201

"we're good buddies", can each be conveyed by the amount of touching permitted.

A look at the data reveals that this is the case. In the bars all "0's" which occurred were between males and females. These were recorded for the groups which tend to touch the most, the Mexicans, Italians, and Greeks. An American couple who were dancing also typify this intensive form of touching. As might be expected, in groups who touch the least, the Polish and Irish, the lowest scores, "1's" and "2's", still index cross-sex interactions. The same can be seen to be the case for the Serbians, Americans, and Germans, who are intermediate on the touch scale. The only place the researchers found this tendency broken was in what Cavan would term a trade bar, where homosexuality was overtly sanctioned. In this case the touching indexes a different social relation, but one no less imbued with cultural significance (cf., Newton 1972). Other cases of same-sex touching inevitably involve different culturally sanctioned role relations. Kinship ties and differential age are most often invoked.

In the church setting the Italians and the Greeks (in that order) display greatest amounts of touching. Among these groups cases of "holding" were observed. A small amount of holding was also observed in the Serbian and Polish groups. The Mexican group did not utilize this touch category ("1"). This may be accounted for by the fact that the ages of the parishioners were generally younger, and no older ladies were present (who touch most often in the church setting). No cases of "prolonged holding" ("0") were recorded in the church setting. In the Italian and Mexican samples there were no instances of a "4" (not touching) recorded. All other groups, including Greek, manifested cases in which 'no contact' occurred. Inasmuch as touching

202

of some sort was generally observed in the Greek community, the instances of no contact recorded may have been accounted for by the fact that the interactants were separated by a doorway. The chi-square value indicates that the differences among groups are significant at the .001 level. Separation of groups by sex indicates that females often do engage in more intimate forms of touching than do males. This is in accord with Sommer's comments on touching (1967: 149). The Americans may be an exception to this generality. Here the only instances of holding ("1") recorded were in cross-sex dyads. Most interactants in the American group were younger couples who did not form the same-sex interaction circles which typified the other church groups. This may have been peculiar to the specific church which had a large parking lot with cars available. In the other churches many of the parishioners were within walking distance of their homes, which contributed to more leisurely departures. No cases of "prolonged holding" ("0") were noted within same-sex dyads in the church setting. This provides support for the contention that the amount of touching serves as a marker of cross-gender interactions for these Indo-European groups.

The chi-square values on all levels of analysis are significant at the .001 level. This variable definitely discriminates between 'touch' and 'non-touch' ethnic groups. Nevertheless, by comparing the church findings with the bar findings no hard and fast normative strategies can be considered typical of any ethnic group in all settings. Rather, the norms change with the context, and this shift is indicated by the test statistics.

On all levels of analysis the observed to expected scores are approximated most closely by the Serbian and American samples. The Germans also approach this expected pattern to an extent, though they tend toward the "non-contact" grouping. All three of these groups are intermediate between what Hall and Watson refer to as "contact" and "non-contact" groups. Both Watson (1970: 85-88) and Hall (1969: 116, 136-38) would place the Americans and Germans unequivocally in the non-contact grouping. In Watson's case this may be an inherent weakness of his experimental design which included no females. When women are added and the situation is allowed to shift of its own accord, the distribution of touching changes concomitantly. Contact and non-contact areas of the world may prove to be a useful contrast, but it is essential to remember that an overall normative pattern for a culture is relatively broad and various ways of communicating information about one's identity are selected in accord with the requirements of a particular setting. The significance of any combination of actions can only be understood in relation to this smaller frame of reference.

204

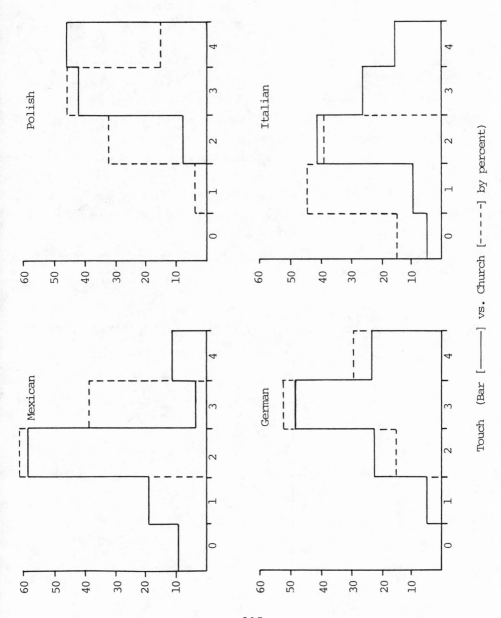

Touch (Bar [————] vs. Church [- - - -] by percent)

205

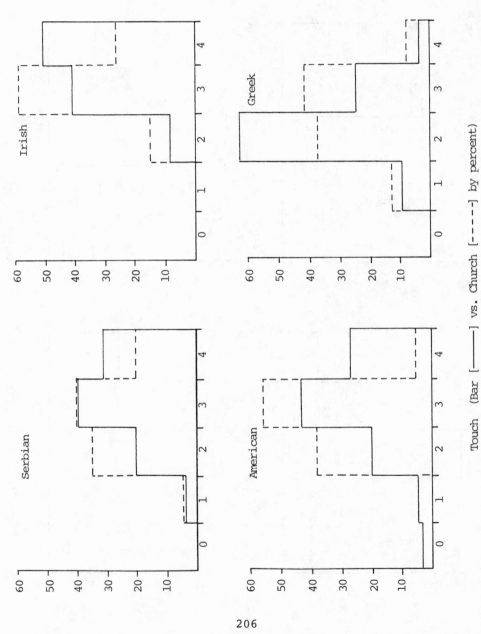

Touch (Bar [——————]) vs. Church [- - - - -] by percent)

Statistical Results for Touch Measure

Using each bar separately:

x^2 = 371.69360   df = 68   sig. = .001

cramer's V = .38345

Bars combined:

x^2 = 232.09416   df = 28   sig. = .001

cramer's V = .30300

Churches:

x^2 = 65.00150   df = 21   sig. = .001

cramer's V = .28019

Ethnic Group	Bar	Time	0	1	2	3	4	
					Measurement Category			
MEXICAN	01	1			4	2		
		2		6	4			
		3		2	4			
		sum		8	12	2		
	11	1			6		2	
		2	2	1	5		2	
		3	3	1	8			
		sum	5	2	19		6	
		tot	5	10	31	2	6	54
POLISH	02	1			2	8		
		2			2	8	4	
		3			1	7	8	
		sum			5	23	12	
	12	1				4	10	
		2				3	9	
		3			1	3	6	
		sum			1	10	25	
		tot			6	33	37	76
GERMAN	04	1			2	2	4	
		3		2	2		2	
		sum		2	4	2	6	
	05	1			6	16	2	
		2			8	4		
		3		2		1	3	
		sum		2	14	21	5	
	15	1				10	6	
		2				8	4	
		3			2	2	4	
		sum			2	20	14	
		tot		4	20	43	25	88
ITALIAN	06	1		2	4			
		2		2	6			
		3		2	2	4		
		sum		6	12	4		
	16	1	2	2	8	6	2	
		2	2		10	6	6	
		3			10	8	6	
		sum	4	2	28	20	14	
		tot	4	8	40	24	14	90

	Bar	Time	\multicolumn{5}{c}{Measurement Category}	
			0	1	2	3	4	
S	07	1				4		
E		2				6	2	
R		3		2	4	4		
B		sum		2	4	14	2	
I	17	1				4	4	
A		2			2		4	
N		3			4	2	6	
		sum			6	6	14	
		tot		2	10	20	16	48
	08	1				6		
		2				2	10	
I		sum				8	10	
R	13	1			3	11	14	
I		2				14	12	
S		3			2	8	10	
H		sum			5	33	36	
	18	1				6	8	
		2			3	3	6	
		3			3	6	9	
		sum			6	15	23	
		tot			11	56	69	136
A	09	1			4	8	4	
M		2	2		2	2	4	
E		3			2	2	8	
R		sum	2		8	12	16	
I	19	1			6	12		
C		2		2	2	4	4	
A		3		1	1	6	2	
N		sum		3	9	22	6	
		tot	2	3	17	34	22	78
G	10	1			4	4		
R		2			6	4	2	
E		3		6	16	2		
E		sum		6	26	10	2	
K	20	1			4			
		2			4	4		
		3			4	2		
		sum			12	6		
		tot		6	38	16	2	62
			11	33	172	229	187	632

Observed / Expected Frequencies

for Touch Measure

ethnic group							
Mexican	B	5 / .9	10 / 2.8	31 / 14.7	2 / 19.6	6 / 16.0	54
	C		0 / 1.6	22 / 12.8	14 / 16.8	0 / 4.8	36
	G	5 / 1.1	10 / 4.5	53 / 26.8	16 / 35.5	6 / 22.2	90
Polish	B	0 / 1.3	0 / 4.0	6 / 20.7	33 / 27.5	37 / 22.5	76
	C		1 / 1.6	12 / 12.8	17 / 16.8	6 / 4.8	36
	G	0 / 1.4	1 / 5.6	18 / 33.3	50 / 44.2	43 / 27.6	112
German	B	0 / 1.5	4 / 4.6	20 / 13.6	43 / 23.9	21 / 26.0	88
	C		0 / 1.5	6 / 12.1	18 / 15.9	10 / 4.6	34
	G	0 / 1.5	4 / 6.0	26 / 36.3	61 / 48.1	31 / 30.1	122
Italian	B	4 / 1.6	8 / 4.7	39 / 14.0	25 / 32.6	14 / 26.6	90
	C		6 / 1.6	16 / 12.8	14 / 16.8	0 / 4.8	36
	G	4 / 1.5	14 / 6.2	55 / 37.5	36 / 49.7	14 / 31.1	126
Serbian	B	0 / .8	2 / 2.5	10 / 13.1	20 / 17.4	16 / 14.2	48
	C		2 / 1.7	14 / 14.2	16 / 18.7	8 / 5.4	40
	G	0 / 1.1	4 / 4.4	24 / 26.2	36 / 34.7	24 / 21.7	88
Irish	B	0 / 2.4	0 / 7.1	11 / 37.0	56 / 49.3	69 / 40.2	136
	C		0 / 1.5	5 / 12.1	20 / 15.9	9 / 4.6	34
	G	0 / 2.1	0 / 8.4	16 / 50.6	76 / 67.0	78 / 41.9	170
American	B	2 / 1.4	3 / 4.1	17 / 21.2	34 / 28.3	22 / 23.1	78
	C		0 / 1.6	14 / 12.8	20 / 16.8	2 / 4.8	36
	G	2 / 1.4	3 / 5.6	31 / 33.9	54 / 44.4	24 / 28.1	114
Greek	B	0 / 1.1	6 / 3.2	38 / 16.9	16 / 22.5	2 / 18.3	62
	C		3 / 1.0	9 / 8.5	10 / 11.2	2 / 3.2	24
	G	0 / 1.0	9 / 4.3	47 / 25.6	26 / 33.9	4 / 21.2	86
bar totals		11	33	172	229	187	632
church totals			12	98	129	37	276
group totals		11	45	270	358	224	908

B = bar   C = church   G = total group

Proxemic variable V: Visual

Amount of eye contact fits well the emerging pattern for the various ethnic groups. The chi-square value is more than high enough to indicate its significance at the .001 level.   The Greeks and Mexicans exhibited the most eye contact in the bar setting, followed closely by the Serbians and Italians.   Both the Serbians and Polish show some significant situational shifts between bars. By looking at the within-group percentages, however, one can see that members of the Polish community use a wide range of eye contact, but they also exhibit the least direct eye contact. They are followed closely by the Germans, while the Serbians are intermediate between the German-Polish group and the more direct eye contact groups.   The Irish and American samples are quite similar in that they exhibit at least a minimal amount of eye contact, though it is never direct ('macular' and 'peripheral' rather than 'foveal'). Situational variations, such as lighting and noise level, have a notable effect on the type of eye contact and on voice loudness.

In the churches the most direct eye contact is manifested by the Greeks, followed by the Italians, Mexicans, and Serbians. In all groups except the Polish and American, 'macular' eye contact is most commonly used in interactions. The Irish were the only group to employ the category 'no eye contact' in the church setting.   The Americans show a strong preference for peripheral eye

211

contact with 66.7% of the interactants utilizing this category. The Polish show an equal preference for either the macular or peripheral categorizations. As in the bars, the American and Irish samples concentrate all of their gaze directions in either the macular or peripheral categories. The German and Polish parishoners also show a preference for this gaze strategy in the church setting. The chi-square value establishes the significance of differences in the churches at the .001 level.

Separating the sample by sex, it is apparent that the women in the Serbian and Italian samples maintain more direct eye contact than do the men (13 versus 23 percent for the Serbians and 10 versus 30 percent for the Italians). In the other cases, preference for eye contact follows the pattern of the ethnic group as a whole and is not significantly different between males and females.

Some difficulties have been encountered in obtaining an accurate measure of the visual variable using Hall's methodology. It has been demonstrated that the visual dimension is closely tied to the speech situation and shifts accordingly in a very precise manner (see Kendon or Duncan). To deal with this the researchers have recorded the situation which is most typical of a dyad at each of the ten minute intervals of measurement. The experimental design of this study thus uses Hall's code to record the general normative patterns that typify stretches of interaction. This record is not as fine-grained as the sort of microscopic transcription which Duncan and Goodwin have done. Indeed, Hall's schema is more suited to recording general trends than it is to identifying momentary shifts in gaze direction or focus. Changes along either of these dimensions may alter the coding with Hall's schema and, if one interactant looks away, the visual measure for both individuals must change. These design features of Hall's code complicate the measurement of minute shifts in gaze direction and focus.

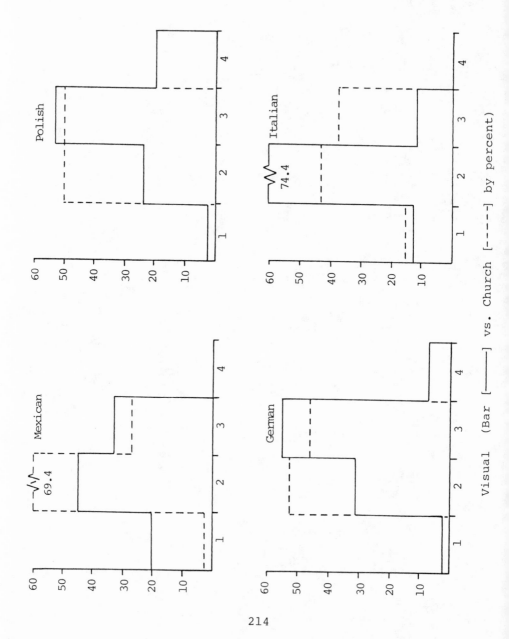

Visual (Bar [———] vs. Church [- - - -] by percent)

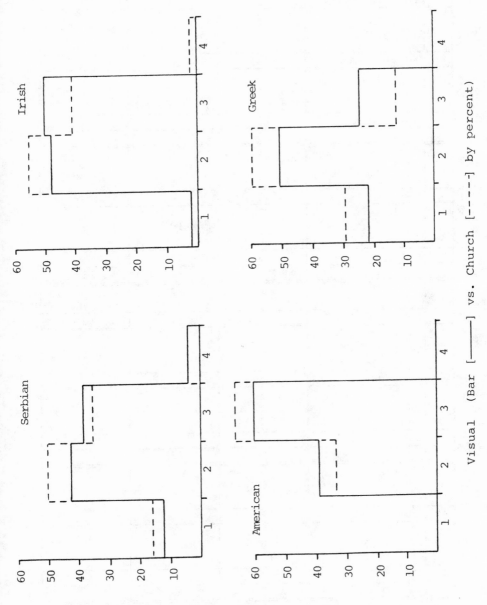

Visual (Bar [——] vs. Church [– – – –] by percent)

215

Visual

Ethnic Group	Bar	Time	Measurement Category			
			1	2	3	4
MEXICAN	01	1		4	2	
		2	6		4	
		3	2	2	2	
		sum	8	6	8	
	11	1		6	2	
		2		6	4	
		3	3	7	4	
		sum	3	19	10	
		tot	11	25	18	54
POLISH	02	1		2	3	5
		2	1	4	5	4
		3	1	7	8	
		sum	2	13	16	9
	12	1		3	7	4
		2			10	2
		3		2	8	
		sum		5	25	6
		tot	2	18	41	15 → 76
GERMAN	04	1	1	3	2	2
		3		3		
		sum	1	6	2	2
	05	1		6	17	1
		2		8	4	
		3	1	2	1	2
		sum	1	16	22	3
	15	1		3	11	2
		2		2	10	
		3	1	2	5	
		sum	1	7	26	2
		tot	3	29	50	7 → 88
ITALIAN	06	1		6		
		2		6	2	
		3	1	6	1	
		sum	1	18	3	
	16	1		16	4	
		2	8	14	2	
		3	3	19	2	
		sum	11	49	8	
		tot	12	67	11	90

216

Visual (continued)

Bar	Time	Measurement Category 1	2	3	4	
S E R B I A N						
07	1	2		2		
	2	2	2	4		
	3	2	6	2		
	sum	6	8	8		
17	1		4	4		
	2		4		2	
	3		5	7		
	sum		13	11	2	
	tot	6	21	19	2	48
I R I S H						
08	1	2	4			
	2		4	8		
	sum	2	8	8		
13	1		12	16		
	2		15	11		
	3		11	9		
	sum		38	36		
18	1		4	10		
	2		6	6		
	3	1	8	9		
	sum	1	18	25		
	tot	3	64	69		136
A M E R I C A N						
09	1		6	10		
	2		3	7		
	3		1	11		
	sum		10	28		
19	1		8	10		
	2		7	5		
	3		6	4		
	sum		21	19		
	tot		31	47		78
G R E E K						
10	1		4	4		
	2		8	4		
	3	6	14	4		
	sum	6	26	12		
20	1	4				
	2	2	6			
	3	2		4		
	sum	8	6	4		
	tot	14	32	16		62
		50	287	271	24	632

Statistical Results for Visual Measure

Using each bar separately:

x^2 = 268.03784   df = 51   sig. = .001

cramer's V = .37599

Bars combined:

x^2 = 188.50854   df = 21   sig. = .001

cramer's V = .31532

Churches:

x^2 = 60.69730   df = 21   sig. = .001

cramer's V = .27075

Observed / Expected Frequencies

for Visual Measure

ethnic group		1	2	3	4	T=
Mexican	B	11 / 4.3	25 / 24.5	18 / 23.2	0 / 2.1	54
	C	1 / 2.6	25 / 18.5	10 / 14.7	0 / .1	36
	G	12 / 6.9	50 / 42.5	28 / 38.1	0 / 2.5	90
Polish	B	2 / 6.0	18 / 34.5	41 / 32.6	15 / 2.9	76
	C	0 / 2.6	18 / 18.5	18 / 14.7	0 / .1	36
	G	2 / 8.6	36 / 52.9	59 / 47.4	15 / 3.1	112
German	B	2 / 7.0	29 / 40.0	50 / 37.7	7 / 3.3	88
	C	0 / 2.5	18 / 17.5	16 / 13.9	0 / .1	34
	G	2 / 9.4	47 / 57.6	66 / 51.6	7 / 3.4	122
Italian	B	12 / 7.1	67 / 40.9	11 / 38.6	0 / 3.4	90
	C	6 / 2.6	16 / 18.5	14 / 14.7	0 / .1	36
	G	18 / 9.7	83 / 59.5	25 / 53.3	0 / 3.5	126
Serbian	B	6 / 3.8	21 / 21.8	19 / 20.6	2 / 1.8	48
	C	6 / 2.9	20 / 20.6	14 / 16.4	0 / .1	40
	G	12 / 6.8	41 / 41.6	33 / 37.2	2 / 2.4	88
Irish	B	3 / 10.8	64 / 61.8	69 / 58.3	0 / 5.2	136
	C	0 / 2.5	19 / 17.5	14 / 13.9	1 / .1	34
	G	3 / 13.1	83 / 80.3	83 / 71.9	1 / 4.7	170
American	B	0 / 6.2	31 / 35.4	47 / 33.4	0 / 3.0	78
	C	0 / 2.6	12 / 18.5	24 / 14.7	0 / .1	36
	G	0 / 8.8	43 / 53.9	71 / 48.2	0 / 3.1	114
Greek	B	14 / 4.9	32 / 28.2	16 / 26.6	0 / 2.4	62
	C	7 / 1.7	14 / 12.3	3 / 9.8	0 / .1	24
	G	21 / 6.6	46 / 40.6	19 / 36.4	0 / 2.4	86
bar totals		50	287	271	24	632
church totals		20	142	113	1	276
group totals		70	429	384	25	908

Proxemic variable VI: Vocal

In the bar setting significant differences are found among ethnic groups comparing along lines of voice loudness (the chi-square value is significant at the .001 level). A look at the chart indicates that the Italians are the loudest, followed by the Greeks and Americans. Surprisingly enough, the Mexican group appear relatively quiet, but the raw frequency chart indicates that this is due mainly to the interactions in bar #11, a case where two unmarried women were present, who significantly affected the tone of interaction. The German groups were the most quiet, along with the remaining American population. In both American bars there was a soft-spoken group in evidence alongside their out-spoken contemporaries. The Polish, Irish, and Serbian samples form an intermediate category, with the Serbian groups being a bit louder. Some between-bar shifts appear in both the Polish and Serbian groups, corresponding to shifts in the other proxemic variables. In the churches the Greeks are preeminently the loudest. While in both the church and bar situations the Greeks have a relatively 'loud' score, the contextual differences can be accounted for, in part, on the basis of gender differences. In the Greek church the "4's" (very loud) are recorded only for women; none of the Greek males use this category. As in the bars, though, neither do any Greeks use the "1" (very soft) category. The Greeks in our sample are followed in loudness by an intermediate series of groups including the Irish, Mexicans, and Italians. Germans show the widest and most

220

balanced range of voice loudness (from complete silence to very loud interactions). This wide range of action typifies the Germans for most of the other measures as well. The Mexicans and Serbians are the only groups which do not make use of the "very loud" category. The Serbians and Polish concentrate their interactions in the "normal" category of voice loudness (90% and 83.3% respectively). In the church setting the chi-square indicates the differences among groups is significant at the .001 level.

Separating the church data by sex, the women are generally louder than the men. The only exception is the Italian women. They provide a situational shift from the case in the Italian bars where the women proved to be much louder than their male counterparts. The Greek women are the loudest, followed by the Irish women and the Polish women. The loudest men are found in the Italian group, followed by the Americans and Germans. As might be expected, a large majority of all cases divided statistically by church and by sex fall into the "normal" or "soft" categories. The extreme cases noted above are not necessarily indicative of any pronounced trends in the group as a whole.

The researchers reduced Hall's vocal code to include only four voice loudness levels for purposes of manage-ability. After extensive use of this code, we believe a six division coding procedure may have been more useful: silent, very soft (whisper), soft, normal, loud, very loud (yelling). Few other problems were encountered in coding this variable. Such things as lighting and overall noise level, as mentioned, have an obvious effect on this variable and deserve notation. Also, Hall seems to have arbitrarily chosen voice loudness as a feature deserving of 'proxemic coding'. There seems little reason to privilege voice loudness over other prosodic and paralinguistic features as being of significance for coding interactions. A more complete recording in conjunction with linguistic transcription is sure to produce richer analyses.

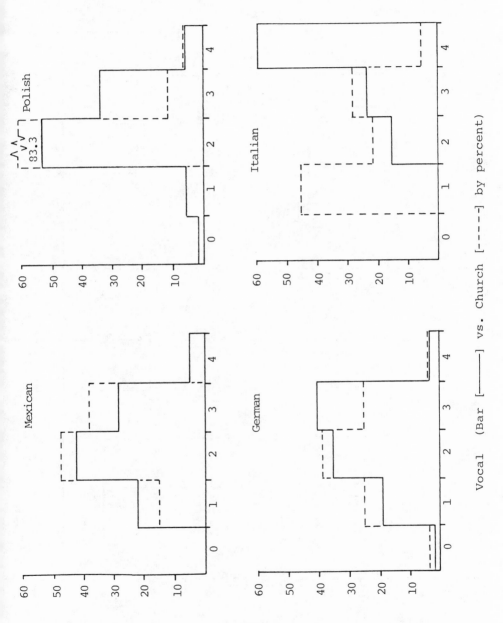

Vocal (Bar [——] vs. Church [- - - -] by percent)

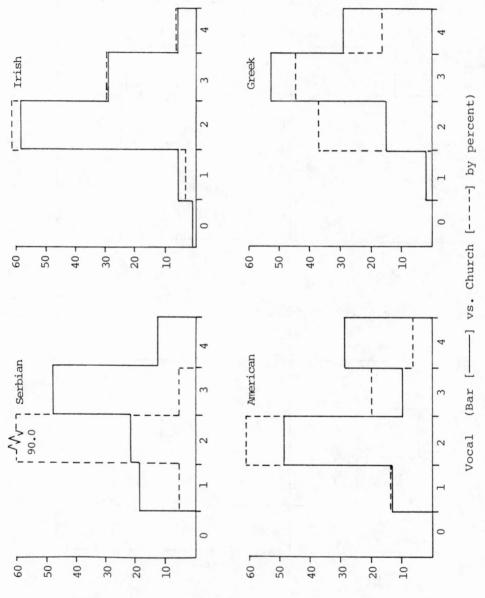

Vocal (Bar [━━━] vs. Church [- - - -] by percent)

Statistical Results for Vocal Measure

Using each bar separately:

x^2 = 354.63184   df = 68   sig. = .001

cramer's V = .37454

Bars combined:

x^2 = 235.80254   df = 28   sig. = .001

cramer's V = .30541

Churches:

x^2 = 101.27104   df = 28   sig. = .001

cramer's V = .30287

Vocal

Ethnic Group	Bar	Time	0	1	2	3	4	
MEXICAN	01	1			4	1	1	
		2		2	1	5	2	
		3		2	2	2		
		sum		4	7	8	3	
	.11	1			1	7		
		2		3	7			
		3		5	9			
		sum		8	17	7		
		tot		12	24	15	3	54
POLISH	02	1	1	1	4	1	3	
		2		1	6	6	1	
		3			8	8		
		sum	1	2	18	15	4	
	12	1			7	7		
		2			8	4		
		3		2	8			
		sum		2	23	11		
		tot	1	4	41	26	4	76
GERMAN	04	1		2	2			
		3	1		1	4		
		sum	1	2	3	4		
	05	1		6	10	8		
		2		3	6	3		
		3		4	1	1		
		sum		13	17	12		
	15	1		1	3	8	4	
		2		1	3	8		
		3			5	3		
		sum		2	11	19	4	
		tot	1	17	31	35	4	88
ITALIAN	06	1					6	
		2					8	
		3			3	3	2	
		sum			3	3	16	
	16	1				12	8	
		2			5	3	16	
		3			6	4	14	
		sum			11	19	38	
		tot			14	22	54	90

226

	Bar	Time	Measurement Category					
			0	1	2	3	4	
S	07	1		2		2		
E		2		4	2	2		
R		3		3	2	4	1	
B		sum		9	4	8	1	
I	17	1			4	4		
A		2			2	3	1	
N		3				8	4	
		sum			6	15	5	
		tot		9	10	23	6	48
I	08	1				2	4	
		2			3	5	4	
		sum			3	7	8	
R	13	1		4	20	4		
I		2	1	2	18	5		
S		3			17	3		
H		sum	1	6	55	12		
	18	1		1	7	6		
		2			4	8		
		3		2	9	6	1	
		sum		3	20	20	1	
		tot	1	9	78	39	9	
A	09	1			8	5	3	
M		2		2	6	1	1	
E		3		3	4		5	
R		sum		5	18	6	9	
I	19	1		2	9	1	6	
C		2		2	6		4	
A		3		2	5		3	
N		sum		6	20	1	13	
		tot		11	38	7	22	78
G	10	1				5	3	
		2				7	5	
R		3			6	11	7	
E		sum			6	23	15	
E	20	1			1	3		
K		2		1	2	4	1	
		3			1	3	2	
		sum		1	4	10	3	
		tot		1	10	33	18	62
			3	63	246	200	120	

227

Observed / Expected Frequencies

for Vocal Measure

ethnic group		0	1	2	3	4	T=
Mexican	B	0 / .3	12 / 5.4	24 / 21.0	15 / 17.1	3 / 10.3	54
	C	0 / .1	5 / 5.0	17 / 20.3	14 / 8.7	0 / 1.8	36
	G	0 / .4	17 / 10.0	41 / 39.8	29 / 26.5	3 / 13.3	90
Polish	B	1 / .4	4 / 7.6	41 / 29.6	26 / 24.1	4 / 14.4	76
	C	0 / .1	0 / 5.0	30 / 20.3	4 / 8.7	2 / 1.8	36
	G	1 / .5	4 / 12.5	71 / 49.6	30 / 32.9	6 / 16.5	112
German	B	1 / .4	17 / 8.8	31 / 34.3	35 / 27.8	4 / 16.7	88
	C	1 / .1	9 / 4.7	13 / 19.2	9 / 8.3	2 / 1.7	34
	G	2 / .5	26 / 13.6	44 / 54.0	44 / 35.8	6 / 18.0	122
Italian	B	0 / .4	0 / 5.4	14 / 35.0	22 / 28.5	54 / 17.1	90
	C	0 / .1	16 / 5.0	8 / 20.3	10 / 24.1	2 / 14.4	36
	G	0 / .6	16 / 14.0	22 / 55.8	32 / 37.1	56 / 18.6	126
Serbian	B	0 / .2	9 / 4.8	10 / 18.7	23 / 15.2	6 / 9.1	48
	C	0 / .1	2 / 5.5	36 / 22.6	2 / 9.7	0 / 2.0	40
	G	0 / .4	11 / 9.8	46 / 38.9	25 / 25.9	6 / 12.9	88
Irish	B	1 / .6	9 / 13.6	78 / 52.9	39 / 43.0	9 / 25.8	136
	C	0 / .1	1 / 4.7	21 / 19.2	10 / 8.3	2 / 1.7	34
	G	1 / .7	10 / 18.9	99 / 75.3	49 / 49.9	11 / 25.1	170
American	B	0 / .4	11 / 7.8	38 / 30.4	7 / 24.7	22 / 14.8	78
	C	0 / .1	5 / 5.0	22 / 20.3	7 / 24.1	2 / 14.4	36
	G	0 / .5	16 / 12.7	60 / 50.5	14 / 33.5	24 / 16.8	114
Greek	B	0 / .3	1 / 6.2	10 / 24.1	33 / 19.6	18 / 11.8	62
	C	0 / .1	0 / 3.3	9 / 13.6	11 / 5.8	4 / 1.2	24
	G	0 / .4	1 / 9.6	19 / 38.1	44 / 25.3	22 / 12.7	86
bar totals		3	63	246	200	120	632
church totals		1	38	156	67	14	276
group totals		4	101	402	267	134	908

B = bar   C = church   G = total group

228

IV

FUTURE DIRECTIONS: RE-READING EDWARD SAPIR

Future Directions: Re-reading Edward Sapir

Reflecting on the accomplishments and limitations of this project leads us closer to understanding the critical importance of culturally-fashioned communications styles. We have been able to show that there are indeed significant differences in the interaction styles of various ethnic groups. This has been accomplished through a research design which allowed for naturalistic observation and eliminated many of the biases of a laboratory situation. We have also demonstrated that situational variations exist in the interaction patterns of each ethnic group and that these variations often reflect identifiable status and role markers that vary from context to context. In this sense the action signifiers encode various pragmatic messages.

In spite of these accomplishments there remain basic problems in the research methodology which have limited the ability to further abstract from the data. The principal problem focuses on this question: "how can one abstract cultural categories and lend appropriate interpretations with a research method that arbitrarily imposes analytic units on data from various cultural groups"? In this study, we have shown that Hall's coding procedure pre-establishes the boundaries, indeed the very existence, of an 'intimate' interaction style along the dimension of 'touch'. In this example, how can one be sure that Hall's category in any way reflects what Greeks or Germans or Italians might consider an 'intimate' form of interaction. In short, seldom, if ever, can one be certain that this is the case.

The problem has two dimensions. First, the problem of defining units of analysis, and second, the problem of assigning

230

appropriate meanings to various congeries of these units. Hall
has assumed that units may be defined in an arbitrary manner,
units which in some way parallel the 'phonemic' units of early
anthropological linguistic study. Hence the designation of his
discipline, proxemics. None-the-less, the units are in all
senses motivated, and as Hall would admit, are derived only from
his American middle class biases. The assignment of designata
which already lend specific cultural interpretations to these
units, close vs. distant, intimate vs. public, etc., only serves
to obscure meanings which a particular cultural group may place
on a situation. The imputation of meaning thus becomes an
exercise in speculative sociology.

To alleviate this problem, we would suggest that future
researchers adopt a perspective which defines units of analysis
on the basis of cultural acceptability, and specifically in terms
of the appropriateness of particular types of actions to
specific situations. What have been termed 'marked cases' in the
above study serve as one sort of delineation of such appropriate
actions. These cases are ones which do not generally fit the
normative pattern of a bar setting or a church setting. But,
unless such actions cause another interactant to feel compelled
to engage in a remedial interchange, these actions fall within a
broad range of activities considered acceptable for that situation. They signify, simultaneously, a whole series of identity
attributes to which others will respond appropriately. Ties of
kinship, age, class, gender, as well as ethnicity, are
differentially encoded in these actions depending upon the
setting of a specific interaction.

Another means of determining appropriate actions is by
violating the expectations for a particular situation. This
generally produces an imbalance in expectations and responses
resulting in embarrassment for someone concerned and requiring
what Goffman terms a remedial interchange. That is, an attempt

231

will be made to re-establish the expected normative pattern by making amends for an inappropriate response. This is a culturally-sensitive way of defining the boundaries that separate appropriate and inappropriate action for a wide array of contrastive contexts. Though in any specific context a range of actions will be acceptable, there are definite limits to this range. Those limits become apparent when a remedial interchange is required.

The type of analysis to be derived from this research strategy would yield more fruitful results in that the categories selected by the anthropologist are meaningful determinants of action for a particular cultural group. Boundaries defined in this manner approximate the categories of action used as signifiers in various social settings. This is not the case with Hall's analytic prox"emic" categories. As mentioned, by opting to use Hall's categories, our analysis is limited to being able to compare various cultural groups along a common scale and to determine general tendencies which may be reflected in one group and not in another. There is no way, given these presuppositions, to relate these analytic categories to the specific cultural meanings imputed to any action by members of the culture. With this approach one cannot legitimately say what an "intimate" interaction distance is for a member of the Chicago Greek ethnic community.

Hall and Watson have complicated this question by making the assumption that all non-verbal actions are outside of the conscious manipulation of members of the culture.[13] The only ones qualified to make judgments concerning the 'meanings' of any action or combination of actions are social analysts who may have little knowledge of the cultural schema. The authors strongly disagree with this unsupported assumption. As with linguistic analysis, various portions of the 'structure' of the non-verbal milieu will be able to be brought to the level of awareness by

232

perceptive members of the cultural group. As discussed above, the cultural representatives will know when unwritten rules have been broken.

More importantly, members of the culture can place an interpretation on any specific series of actions and will be able to reflect on how those actions might be different if various aspects of the social situation were in fact different. As with lexical items in the verbal domain, the members of the culture will likely have more awareness of what particular conglomerations of actions are intended to 'mean' than they will of how the units are structured.

The authors would thus suggest that the best manner in which to obtain the boundaries of culturally significant units is through a process of contextual comparisons and marked cases (actions which are considered appropos in a setting by their reflection of role relations which supersede the specifications of the situation). The best manner in which to begin to impute meanings to various action strategies is to ask members of the culture what their interpretation of the meaning of specific actions may be. Queries should then be made as to how that interpretation would change if the interactant were male rather than female, child rather than adult, an outsider rather than a member of the local community, etcetera. Each of these sorts of questions would bring a great deal of taken-for-granted knowledge to the awareness of the members of any ethnic community.

The result would be a series of culturally sensitive units which relate actions to social contexts. These units can then be formalized in an explicit fashion by the social analyst. In addition, one would have a series of what Silverstein (personal communication) terms ethnometapragmatic statements: statements that reflect indigenous notions of what each person believes various action strategies try to communicate. These statements

233

are not the final end product of analysis. They do not comprise the dictionary of motivations of action, though they are the key to such a dictionary. To give such statements an explanatory power in and of themselves would be a positivist error. It would reduce complex semiotic constructions to a one-to-one relation between a particular interpretation of a action sequence (a token) and an abstract type derived from a large array of specific instances.

Many of the indigenous statements will be referable to a minute contextual analyses, resulting in a more refined pragmatic 'grammar'. Other statements will prove to be variations of essentially similar interpretations, referable to the pragmatic grammar through a series of rules which operate on the semantical plane. Finally, some statements will be erroneous, not in that they do not fit within the range of possible cultural constructions, but in that they represent a misinterpretation of the specific situation in the domain of social action.

The sort of research strategy we are proposing relates non-verbal units to the linguistic dimension, to the social milieu, and to the cultural domain, which are perhaps separable only in analytic terms. This type of multi-dimensioned approach allows the researcher to incorporate a notion of meaningfully related units of action into an analytic framework. Unlike Hall's schema, the units are derived through contextual comparison within specific cultures. At the highest levels of abstraction the units may prove to have a cross-cultural relevance, but in order to remain sensitive to culturally nuanced meaning, the analyst must begin with contextually and culturally relative units to avoid arbitrary analytic unit definitions.

This sort of analysis supersedes Hall's speculative sociology, his construction of a text that includes what Leach has termed "tendentious misleading hunches" (1968). It is the

234

incorporation of a notion of culturally significant action that begins to unravel the unwritten code about which Sapir speculates:

A very good example of another field for the development of unconscious cultural patterns is that of gesture. Gestures are hard to classify and it is difficult to make a conscious separation between that in gesture which is of merely individual origin and that which is referable to the habits of the group as a whole. In spite of these difficulties of conscious analysis, we respond to gestures with an extreme alertness and, one might almost say, in accordance with an elaborate and secret code that is written nowhere, known by none, and understood by all. But this code is by no means referable to simple organic responses. On the contrary, it is as finely certain and artificial, as definitely a creation of social tradition, as language or religion or industrial technology. Like everything else in human conduct, gesture roots in the reactive necessities of the organism, but the laws of gesture, the unwritten code of gestured messages and responses, is the anonymous work of an elaborate social tradition. Whoever doubts this may soon become convinced when he penetrates into the significance of gesture patterns of other societies than his own (Sapir 1927).

Sapir's writings were visionary, searching for new domains to which his knowledge might be applied. Yet they were also pervaded by a sense of caution, afraid to place too much weight on anthropology's own unstable ontology. Heckled by the remnants of nineteenth-century modes of inquiry, uncertain of the relation between the individual and society, hampered by a limited range of analytic tools, Sapir nonetheless perceived essential differeces in the significance of actions to representatives of various cultures. As a sort of tribute to

235

Sapir, Hall, at times, has been able to emulate and extend Sapir's imaginative scenarios. But he has encumbered these insights with the trappings of misapplied metaphors from anthropological linguistics and animal ethology.

The present work attempts to fill a gap; it uses some currents of anthropological thought to bridge the chasm created between methodologies aimed at tracing gross level cultural differences and newer approaches that seek the specific shapes, the contents, and multiply constituted forms of a culture. It returns us, in part, to Sapir's initial line of inquiry, for he ends his quote with a dictum that feminists, Freudians, and anthropologists would each find informative. He suggests the male investigator will be convinced of the social and historical nature of the "unwritten code of gestured messages and responses...when he penetrates into the significance of gesture patterns of other societies than his own." Hall has chosen to concentrate on the unwritten code, and, as we have argued, a culturally sensitive code is a critical analytic component that Sapir included in his formula. But there are other threads to Sapir's thought that went unnoticed by Hall. Most critical are those that Sapir used to stitch cultural meaning (what he terms 'significance') into his theory. Indeed, it was meaning that provided the key to varied social forms. We have shown earlier that Sapir was, indeed, extending a linguistic metaphor to the non-verbal domain, but not by a naive transfer of unit distinctions (as does Hall). Instead, he uses meaning as a tool to reveal significant form in his discussion of phonemic shapes, and suggests insightfully (above) that the significance to form metaphor be extended to non-verbal studies as well. Finally, for the first generation of American anthropologists, 'tradition' involved a sense of history, and Sapir was opening up the possibility of multivalent studies of gestural significance by reference to it.

236

Of course there are other ways Sapir's quotation must be read. Sapir was attuned to the way gestural studies lay at the intersection of societies and selves, and the aggressively masculine symbolism he uses, penetration, aptly situates the entire endeavor, potentially, as a sort of cultural and personal inquiry without consent. Indeed, for all societies where the concept of the individual becomes critical, non-verbal studies have the potential to become an invasion of personal privacy. Undoubtedly some of the popularist flair of Hall's writing derives from the way he draws the reader from the "public" to the "private", and then into his vision of the workings of the "intimate" sphere. He uses metaphors of mystification to occlude the study of non-verbal interaction and reinforce the reader's voyeuristic feelings. The very lack of any systematic data analysis to link his surmisings with a body of field research increases the mystique of Hall's endeavor and places it within the realm of the palm reader and outside of the methodological grasp of social investigation. The suggestion that behavioral codes are outside of conscious thought not only reinforces the methodology gap, it lends a final formulaic flair that convinces undiscerning readers that the information found within the pages of this anthropological document are hidden truths that even a most familiar friend might not (be able to) reveal.

But what gets penetrated in Sapir's formula are pattern significances, a metaphor with a female tinge that his literary and anthroplogical colleague Ruth Benedict would develop a few years later (Benedict 1934). Indeed the patterns metaphor has become a core anthropological symbol, and with it has come negative as well as positive yield. Perhaps most misleading is its tendency to convey an extantness, as if events were preconstituted and could be read from outside (even a very sophisticated article like Geertz' Balinese cockfight maintains this illusion [1972]). The current work is only partially successful at reintroducing events to temporality. We

237

successfully show that interactions are processes and significances are contextual. Future studies, however, must continue to concentrate on developing tools to monitor better the ways in which messages are encoded, transmitted, and interpreted, not only as signifiers in what Birdwhistell calls the "body behavioral stream", but as parts of communicative events.

GLOSSARY

allophone - A non-significant variant of a phoneme (Clark et. al. 1985).

alloproxes - proxemic analogues of allophones for Watson; units of action at the equivalent of the phonemic level with different body behavioral shape but with equal 'phonemic' significance.

anomaly - significant divergence in the 'fit' between a paradigm or theory and that which the paradigm models (Kuhn 1962: 82 et. seq.).

characterizing sign - characterizes the signified either by sharing aspects of the signified (as with an iconic signifier) or by arbitrarily representing the signified in accord with cultural convention (a rule) (as with a symbol).

complementary distribution - the converse of 'free variation' in which two or more allophones of a phoneme occur in a particular phonetic environment, thus, an instance when two allophones of the same phoneme occur in one or more positions where the other is not found (after Clark et. al. 1985).

context - an outline of the preceding and co-occuring events or features that help shape an action or event.

emic - a model of a culture or a unit thereof that attempts to reflect the categories and rules of members of that society. (cf., phonemic)

ethology - the systematic study of animal behavior.

etic - a model of a culture based on analytic units that need not be the same as the units and rules used by members of a society. But note the false analogy with "phonetic" units which, as an ideal type, incorporate all phonemic units used by the members of all linguistic groups.

function - a theory about the interrelatedness of, and causal sequences that link, signifiers (thoughts, events, and actions).

239

icon - a sign vehicle that is tied to the thing or idea that it represents by sharing qualities with that which is represented. A firstness for Peirce (cf., footnote 3).

index - a sign vehicle that 'points to' the thing or idea represented. A secondness for Peirce (cf., footnote 3).

indexicality - a situation in which messages are communicated using indexes.

intersubjectivity - understandings that are mediated or negotiated amongst the participants in any communications situation.

kineme - the smallest contrastive kinesic units that are recognized by the users of that particular kinesic code. The kinesic analogues of phonemes.

kinesics - the study of body behavioral communication.

markedness - two term contrasts where one term is positive (or marked) and the other is neutral (or unmarked) (Lyons 1968: 79).

paradigm - "universally recognized scientific achievements that for a time provide model problems and solutions to a community of practitioners" (Kuhn 1962: viii). A comprehensive theory or model used for purposes of interpretation.

phonemics - the study of the sound units of a language which are distinctive to the members of a culture.

pragmatic - the study of context-dependent meanings; often a part of linguistic 'sense' rather than 'reference' (formal logical or semantic meaning).

proxemic - the study of how various cultures communicate through the use of significant spatial arrangements.

remedial interchange - an activity directed toward restoring an acceptable definition of one's own self when one feels that others are not defining that self in an suitable manner (Goffman 1971: Ch. IV).

residual category - a class of unexplained information that remains after analysis has been completed.

semantic - an analysis of the formal logical meanings of signifiers and strings of signifiers.

semiosis - processes of encoding, transmitting, and decoding, communicated messages.

semiotic - a mode of analysis that rests on the interdependence of the syntactic, semantic, and pragmatic components of any communications situation.

signifier - a type of sign that is used to refer to something else.

signified - the referent of a signifier. The "something else" that is referred to by a signifier, be it an object, an object class, or an idea.

sign vehicle - cf., signifier.

situation - here used synonymously with "context".

structure - an analytic model of the formal organization or pattern that underlies language or culture.

sui generis - 'of its own kind'.

symbol - a signifier that represents the signified arbitrarily, as established solely by a cultural rule.

syntactic - the structural dimension of a language; its grammar. The form of the words in a language and "the manner of their combination in phrases, clauses, and sentences" (Lyons 1968: 54).

with - the parties involved in an interaction.

ENDNOTES

1. While significant sections of this book critique the work of E. T. Hall and O. Michael Watson, we owe them thanks for the textual guidance and promising lines of inquiry they provided.

2. Sapir's articulation of this idea is brought out more clearly in other places. In Language he states that "context, that ground of mutual understanding...is essential to the complete intelligibility of all speech (1949: 92). His discussion of concrete and relational concepts also provide evidence for the semiotic understanding of language that he held (1949: 100-119).

3. We derive our notion of indexicality from Peirce's Tricotomy of Signs. As he states (1932: 156), "A sign, or Representamen, is a First which stands in such a genuine triadic relation to a Second, called its Object, as to be capable of determining a Third, called its Interpretant, to assume the same triadic relation to its Object in which it stands itself to the same Object." He proceeds to define Icons, Indices, and Symbols as follows:

A. "An Icon is a Representamen whose Representative Quality is a Firstness of it as a First. That is, a quality that it has qua thing renders it fit to be a representamen. Thus, anything is fit to be a substitute for anything that it is like" (1932, 157).

B. "An Index or Seme is a Representamen whose Representative character consists in its being an individual second. If the Secondness is an existential relation, the Index is genuine. If the Secondness is a reference, the Index is degenerate. A genuine Index and its Object must be existent individuals (whether things or facts), and its immediate Interpretant must be of the same character. But since every individual must have characters, it follows that a genuine Index may contain a Firstness, and so an Icon as a constituent part of it. Any individual is a degenerate index of its own characters" (1932: 160).

C. "A Symbol is a Representamen whose Representative character consists precisely in its being a rule that will determine its Interpretant. All words, sentences, books, and other conventional signs are Symbols. We speak of writing or pronouncing the word "man"; but it is only a replica, or embodiment of the word, that is pronounced or written. The word itself has no existence although it has a real being, consisting in the fact

242

that existents _will_ conform to it.   It is a general mode of
succession of three sounds or representamens of sounds which
becomes a sign only in the fact that a habit, or acquired law
will cause replicas of it to be interpreted as meaning a man or
men.   The word and its meaning are both general rules; but the
word alone of the two prescribes the qualities of its replicas in
themselves.   Otherwise the 'word' and its 'meaning' do not
differ, unless some special sense be attached to 'meaning'"
(1932: 165-66).

     Closely related to Peirce's formulation are the distinctions
made by G. H. Mead among gestures, "symbols", and significant
symbols: only the latter equates to Peirce's "symbol".   While
both views are pragmatic, Mead's formulation tends toward an
inherent behaviorism.   C. W. Morris' work, Foundations of the
Theory of Signs maintains this behavioristic bias though in an
adumbrated form, while Goffman (Behavior in Public Places [p.
13-15]) uses much less precise language to address similar
questions about the relations between signifiers, signifieds, and
the derivable meanings given cultural rules, specific
interactions, and interpretants.

4. Our appraisal of Hall may appear overly critical, but Leach's
comments in the New York Review of Books (1968: 16-18) are far
more devastating.   Leach considers Hall "a home-grown, very
old-fashioned, practical-problem kind of American anthropologist
who has been quite unaffected by the developments which have
taken place either in his own subject or in linguistics during
the past twenty-five years. ...Dr. Hall, using a crude version
of the now hackneyed analogy that 'culture is like a language',
wants to tell us that our modes of thinking are delimited by our
general cultural experience and that this inhibits us from
understanding members of other cultures.

     "Dr. Hall makes the astonishing claim that 'only in recent
years, and to just a handful of people, have the implications of
Whorf's thinking become apparent'."   Leach disagrees, pointing
out that the general ideas espoused by Whorf were formulated in
Europe a few years earlier by Wittgenstein, and that the basic
tenets of this position have been around at least since the time
of Immanual Kant. As Leach says, "Whorf's thinking has now been
rehashed in so many different forms that it is positively
threadbare."

     Leach seriously questions the ethnographic legitimacy of
Hall's claims, poking a bit of fun at Hall's contentions that
American diplomats who mask their breath may be more offensive to
their Arab counterparts than an announced embargo on oil imports
since the act is a way of "communicating shame".   Hall's comments
about the cramped quarter of French automobiles being compatible
with the "stepped up sensory inputs" of French men and women who
are "sensually involved with one another" catch Leach's eye; but

as ethnographic "facts" they prove less amusing. As he says, Hall "does his profession a disservice by suggesting that the 'science' of anthropology consists of nothing better than the tendentious misleading hunches with which these volumes are filled." Leach ends with an automotive touche: "I must assure him [Dr. Hall] that the unneighborly, unsensual Englishman's favorite car is one of the smallest in the world."

5. After the present study, Hall published his Handbook for Proxemic Research. While the code proposed in this working manual reflect some significant improvements and much more detail (Hall 1974: 41 et seq.), we could not incorporate these into this work ex post facto. The Handbook records some results of empirical research -- Hall's first attempt to substantiate earlier proxemic claims (now, many years later, what seems to be his last word on proxemic research). In the work, he makes some suggestive comments on context and meaning and, following the lead of Watson and the model of Morris, Hall finally realizes that semiotics may provide a working model that can make sense out of proxemic materials (1974: 20-21). While maintaining a loyality to his conscious/unconscious distinction, he goes so far as to suggest that the fieldworker ought to obtain "an inventory of conscious proxemic signs of recognized meaning as an adjunct to other proxemic data" (1974: 20). Thus, while the all-knowing anthropologist is still required to demystify ethnographic knowledge, he or she is no longer its sole source. In seeing proxemics happen, Hall, in the guise of fieldworker, has become less sacred. Cultural competence has been found amidst the masses! Doing serious ethnography thus seems to have benefitted Dr. Hall. Moreover, with the assistance of Jan Washburn Byler, Hall developed a series of statistical tests far more suited to the analysis of proxemic variables than Watson's "t-tests". His preliminary results are provocative. Nonetheless, Hall seems more comfortable in an oracular guise, a position compromised by muddling in field research and analysis. So ongoing research falls to others. We hope the present study, much like the exploratory findings reported in Hall's Handbook, helps revolutionize the study of interaction in a Kuhnian manner -- by pointing up details for which speculative musings like those in Hall's early works are unable to account.

6. We are by no means trying to discredit all of Whorf's work. Indeed, much of his earlier research is conducted in a precise descriptive manner that allows allow other specialists to reevaluate his ideas about cultural variability from an ethnographic point of view as well as in terms of how they relate to cognition. Whorf's earlier articles, "Grammatical Categories" and "Some Verbal Categories of Hopi" are excellent in this regard. As Silverstein notes, they contrast rather sharply with his later work such as "Science and Linguistics" or "Language, Mind, and Reality". The essential difference between the earlier and later works is in the degree of relationship that is proposed

244

between linguistic categories and thought: early on Whorf suggests a _limiting_ relationship while his later works tend toward a _causal_ link. Hall's citations make it clear that he is undiscriminating in his use of Whorf. As we suggest, at times Hall even implies that neither language nor culture may be factors in determining the sensory shapes that humans enact (see footnote 7).

7. Leach agrees that, taken literally, Hall's theory reduces to a form of racism or, as he terms it, "racialism": "The reader is given some misleading information about the role of competition in evolution, and is offered the implicitly racialist suggestion that differences of culture in man are closely analogous to differences of species in animals. This cardinal error recurs at various places throughout the book: cultural labels are used like species labels, and the fact that a single individual may...radically change his culture several times over in (sic.) the course of a single lifetime is completely ignored" (1968: 16).

8. As is readily apparent, even this single statement contains an unacceptable amount of semantic ambiguity: Hall states that man (humans at the species level, one presumes) has a uniform way of handling distance; in the same breath, he contends that two means of coping with spatial relations have been eliminated (or "screened" at least), obviously by the "advent" of culture.

9. The whole idea of "objective" research deserves further attention. The subjective versus objective opposition is used in the sense in which Weber referred to it, but it can be traced back through Marx to Hegel and Kant, then further to the differentiation in western civilizations between body and mind. It reappears in Schutz, G. H. Mead (H. S. Sullivan in psychology) and Goffman, and the same distinction surface once more in Birdwhistell's differentiation between overt and covert (1970: 240). While the measures we are taking are amenable to "objective" analysis of the sort Weber describes, any semiotic consideration must take into account the intersubjective nature of communications acts. The ethnographic sketches seek to make the intersubjective formulation of mediated meanings more apparent.

10. At all three of these levels the specific times of measurement have been combined. At the bar level, all bars studied within a particular ethnic group have been combined. This 'combined' figure appears on the expected frequency table, whereas the specific time measurements can be found on the raw data tables. 'Group' is a combination of bar and church scores for each ethnic population.

11. In a footnote to a more recent piece, Watson noted that he has received criticism for treating his data as interval. "To

statistical purists let me say that I'm well aware that I have applied interval tests on data that were for the most part ordinal. There were several reasons for doing this..." (1972: 13). We do not feel we are statistical purists, but rather followers of very basic assumptions that lend legitimacy to specific statistical procedures. Non-parametric tests were developed for just our type of data and are therefore much more adequate than basic "T-tests" (Blalock 1972; Siegel 1956).

12. Looking at the Kruskal-Wallis test, the individual test statistics (Ri) allow one to easily rank the ethnic groups for comparison on that particular measure. For comparisons between contexts (bars and churches) the percentage graphs following each measure are the most useful.

13. For a further consideration of consciousness see G. H. Mead (1962: 30-31).

BIBLIOGRAPHY

Benedict, Ruth
   1934 <u>Patterns of Culture</u>. Boston: Houghton Mifflin.

Berlin, Brent and Paul Kay
   1969 <u>Basic Color Terms: Their Universality and
       Evolution.</u> Berkeley: University of California
       Press.

Birdwhistell, Ray L.
   1969 <u>Kinesics and Context</u>. Philadelphia: University of
       Pennsylvania Press.

   1972 "Review of <u>Proxemic Behavior</u>, by O. Michael Watson,
       in <u>American Anthropologist</u> 74 (4): 830-31.

Blakely, Thomas
   1983 "To Gaze or Not to Gaze: Visual Communication in
       Eastern Zaire," in <u>Case Studies in the Ethnography
       of Speaking</u>, R. Bauman and J. Sherzer (eds.).
       Austin: S. W. Ed. Dev. Lab.

Blalock, Hubert M., Jr.
   1972 <u>Social Statistics</u>. New York: McGraw Hill Company.

Boas, Franz
   1940 "Race and Progress," in <u>Race, Language, and Culture</u>.
       New York: The Free Press.

Brownlee, K. A.
   1965 <u>Statistical Theory and Methodology in Science and
       Engineering</u>. New York: Wiley.

Burgess, Ernest W., and Charles Newcomb, eds.
   1931 <u>Census Data of the City of Chicago, 1920</u>. Chicago:
       The University of Chicago Press.

   1933 <u>Census Data of the City of Chicago, 1930</u>. Chicago:
       The University of Chicago Press.

Cavan, Sherri
   1966 <u>Liquor License; An Ethnography of Bar Behavior</u>.
       Chicago: Aldine Publishing Company.

247

City of Chicago
  1963 <u>An Atlas of Chicago's People, Jobs, and Homes</u>.
        Chicago: Community Renewal Program.

Clark, Virginia P., P. A. Eschholz and A. F. Rosa
  1985 <u>Language: Introductory Readings</u>. New York: St.
        Martin's Press.

Clifford, James
  1983 "On Ethnographic Authority," <u>Representations</u> vol. 1
        (number 2): 118-146.

Condon, W. S. and W. D. Ogston
  1966 "Sound Film Analysis of Normal and Pathological
        Behavior Patterns." <u>Journal of Nervous and Mental
        Disease,</u> vol. 143.

Conklin, Harold C.
  1955 "Hanunoo Color Categories," <u>Southwestern Journal of
        Anthropology</u>, vol. 11: 339-44.

Duncan, Starkey, Jr.
  1969 "Nonverbal Communication," <u>Psychological Bulletin</u>,
        vol. 72 (number 2): 118-137.

  1972 "Some Signals and Rules for Taking Speaking Turns in
        Conversations," <u>Journal of Personality and Social
        Psychology</u>, vol. 23 (number 2): 283-292.

Eakins, Barbara and Gene Eakins
  1978 <u>Sex Differences in Human Communication</u>. Boston:
        Houghton Mifflin.

Fishman, Pamela
  1983 "Interaction: the Work Women Do," in <u>Language
        Gender, and Society,</u> B. Thorne, C. Kramare, and N.
        Henly, (eds.). Rowley, Massachusetts: Newbury
        Publishers.

Geertz, Clifford
  1972 "Deep Play: Notes on the Balinese Cockfight,"
        <u>Daedalus</u> 101: 1-37.

Goffman, Erving
  1959 <u>The Presentation of Self in Everyday Life</u>. New
        York: Doubleday and Company.

  1963 <u>Behavior in Public Places</u>. New York: The Free
        Press.

  1971 <u>Relations in Public</u>. New York: Harper and Row.

Goodenough, Ward H.
1965 "Rethinking 'Status' and 'Role': Toward a General
       Model of Cultural Organization of Social
       Relationships," in The Relevance of Models for
       Social Anthropology, Michael Banton(ed.), London:
       Tavistock Publications.

Goodwin, Charles
1981 Conversational Organization: Interaction between
       Speakers and Hearers. New York: Academic Press.

Goodwin, Marjorie H.
1980 "he-said-she-said: formal cultural procedures for
       the construction of a gossip dispute activity,"
       American Ethnologist volume 7 (number 4).

1982 "process of dispute management among urban black
       children," American Ethnologist volume 9 (number
       1).

Greenberg, Joseph H. (ed.)
1966 Universals of Language. Cambridge, Massachusetts:
       M. I. T. Press.

Hall, Edward T.
1959 The Silent Language. New York: Doubleday and
       Company.

1963 "A System for the Notation of Proxemic Behavior,"
       American Anthropologist, vol. 65.

1968 "Proxemics," Current Anthropology, vol. 9 (number
       2-3).

1969 The Hidden Dimension. New York: Doubleday and
       Company.

1974 Handbook for Proxemic Research. Washington, D.C.:
       Society for the Anthropology of Visual
       Communication.

Hochschild, Arlie R.
1983 The Managed Heart: Commercialization of Human
       Feeling. Berkeley: University of California Press.

Hunter, Albert
1974 Symbolic Communities. Chicago: The University of
       Chicago Press.

Kendon, Adam
1967 "Some Functions of Gaze Direction in Social
       Interaction," Acta Psychologica, vol. 26.

249

Kuhn, Thomas S.
   1962   The Structure of Scientific Revolutions. Chicago:
          University of Chicago Press.

Labov, William and D. Fanshell
   1977   Theraputic Discourse: Psychotherapy as
          Conversation. New York: Academic Press.

Leach, Edmund
   1968   "Nonsense and Sensibility," The New York Review of
          Books, volume X (#10): 16-18.

Lyons, John
   1968   Introduction to Theoretical Linguistics. Cambridge:
          Cambridge University Press.

Mead, George Herbert
   1962   Mind, Self and Society. Chicago: University of
          Chicago Press.

Morris, Charles W.
   1938   Foundations of the Theory of Signs. Chicago:
          University of Chicago Press.

Newton, Esther
   1979   Mother Camp: Female Impersonators in America.
          Chicago: University of Chicago Press.

Park, Robert E.
   1952   Human Communities. New York: The Free Press.

   1967   "The City: Suggestions for the Investigation of
          Human Behavior in the Urban Environment," in The
          City, R. E. Park, E. W. Burgess and R. D. McKenzie.
          Chicago: University of Chicago Press.

Parsons, Talcott
   1937   The Structure of Social Action. New York: The Free
          Press.

Peirce, Charles S.
   1932   Collected Papers of C. S. Peirce, Volume II.
          Cambridge, Massachussetts: Harvard University
          Press.

Ricoeur, Paul
   1970   Freud and Philosophy; an essay on interpretation.
          New Haven: Yale University Press.

Sapir, Edward
  1949 Selected Writings of Edward Sapir, D. G. Mandelbaum
        (ed.). Berkeley: University of California Press.

Schutz, Alfred
  1967 The Phenomenology of the Social World. Evanston:
        Northwestern University Press.

Seigel, Sidney
  1956 Nonparametric Statistics for the Behavioral
        Sciences. New York: McGraw Hill.

Silverstein, Michael
  1973 "Linguistics and Anthropology," in Linguistik und
        die Nachbarwiessenchaften, T. Vennemann and R.
        Bartsch (eds.). Fisher Verlag.

Sommer, R.
  1967 "Small Group Ecology," Psychological Bulletin, vol.
        67 (number 2): 145-152.

Tambiah, Stanley
  1973 "Forms and Meaning of Magical Acts," in Modes of
        Thought: Essays on Thinking in Western and Non-
        Western Societies, R. Horton (ed.). London: Faber.

Thomas, W. I.
  1966 On Social Organization and Social Personality.
        Chicago: University of Chicago Press.

Trager, George L.
  1964 "Paralanguage: A First Approximation," in Language
        in Culture and Society, D. Hymes (ed.). New York:
        Harper and Row.

Turner, Victor
  1969 The Ritual Process. Chicago: Aldine Publishing
        Company.

  1970 "Introduction," Forms of Symbolic Action.
        Proceedings of the 1969 Meeting of the American
        Ethnological Society. Seattle: University of
        Washington Press.

Watson, O. Michael
  1970 Proxemic Behavior. The Hague: Mouton.

  1972a "Conflicts and Directions in Proxemic Research," The
        Journal of Communication, vol. 22: 443-59.

Watson, O. Michael
  1972b "Symbolic and Expressive Uses of Space: an
        Introduction to Proxemic Behavior," <u>McCaleb Module
        in Anthropology</u>. Addison-Wesley; 1-18.

Watson, O. Michael and T. D. Graves
  1966 "Quantitative Research in Proxemic Behavior,"
        <u>American Anthropologist</u>, vol. 68.

Whiting, John and Beatrice B. Whiting
  1970 "Methods for Observing and Recording Behavior,' in
        <u>Handbook of Methods in Cultural Anthropology</u>, R.
        Naroll and R. Cohen, (eds). Garden City, New
        Jersey: Natural History Press.

Whorf, Benjamin L.
  1942 "Language, Mind, and Reality," appears in <u>Language,
        Thought, and Reality</u>, J. B. Carroll (ed.).
        Cambridge, Massachussets: M. I. T. Press; 1956.

INDEX

Ad art, 44, 116, 121
American, 169-170, 203-204;
  bars, 133-142, 162-163, 167-168, 170, 172, 185-186, 202, 211, 220;
  church, 143-145, 171, 186-188, 203, 211-212, 221
Ardrey, Robert, 21
Assyrian, 36

Barone's Bar, 91-100
Bars, viii-xiv, 30-39, 44-56, 130, 160, 162-163, 170-172, 202, 231;
  American, 133-142, 162-163, 167-168, 170, 172, 185-186, 202, 211, 220;
  Children in, 73-74, 83, 147;
  German, 73-87, 92, 162-163, 166, 168, 170, 172, 185-186, 202, 211, 220-221;
  Greek, 146-154, 162-163, 167-170, 172, 185-186, 202, 211, 220;
  Irish, 116-129, 162-163, 167-168, 170, 172, 186-188, 202, 211, 220;
  Italian, 77, 84, 91-100, 105, 162, 166, 168, 170, 172, 185-186, 202, 211, 220-221;
  men in, 41, 44-46, 50-53, 59-61, 66, 73-74, 77-78, 82-83, 91-92, 96-97, 104-105, 116-117, 121-122, 125, 133-134, 138-139, 146-147, 151;
  Mexican, 44-56, 65, 77, 84, 162, 166, 168, 170,172, 185-186, 202, 211, 220;
  Polish, 44, 59-71, 116, 162-163, 166, 168, 170, 172, 185-186, 202, 211, 220;
  Serbian, 104-112, 162-163, 167-168, 170, 172, 186, 202, 211, 220;
  women in, 40, 50-53, 60-61, 73-74, 77-78, 83, 91-92, 96-97, 104, 116-117, 125, 133-134, 138-139, 146-147, 160, 220-221

Benedict, Ruth, 237
Berlin, Brent and Paul Kay, 26

Birdwhistell, Ray L., 4-5, 7, 10, 17, 23-24, 185, 238
Blacks, 34, 105, 138
Blarney Stone Bar, 117-124
Boas, Franz, 18-19
Burgess, Ernest and Charles Newcomb, xiii

Cavan, Sherri, 37, 202
Chi-square, 160-161, 163, 169, 171, 185, 203, 211-212, 220-221
Children, in bars, 73-74, 83, 147
Children, in churches, 143, 155-156
Churches, viii-xiv, 10, 30, 32-36, 38-39, 57-58, 102, 130-131, 144, 160, 163-164, 170-172, 231;
  American, 143-145, 171, 186-188, 203, 211-212, 221;
  German, 71, 88-90, 143, 171, 186-188, 202, 211, 221;
  Greek, 71, 155-157, 171, 186-188, 202-203, 211, 220-221;
  Irish, 130-133, 171, 186-187, 211-212, 221;
  Italian, 101-103, 163, 186-188, 202, 211, 221;
  Men in, 71, 88-89, 102, 130-131, 144, 187-188, 221;
  Mexican, 57-58, 113, 171, 186, 202, 211;
  Polish, 44, 71-72, 156, 171, 186-188, 201, 211-212, 221;
  Serbian, 113-115, 171, 186-188, 201, 211;
  Women in, 71, 88-89, 101-102, 130-131, 143-144, 155-156, 188, 202, 221
Class, xiii, 27, 130, 143, 185-186, 231
Coding, viii, 2-3, 8-10, 14-16, 26-27, 30-31, 37, 39-41, 52-53, 57, 66, 71, 78, 88, 92, 96-97, 102, 105-106, 113, 117, 122, 125-126, 133-134, 138-139, 143-144, 147, 155-156, 159, 162, 171-173, 184, 186-187, 201-202, 212, 221-222, 230, 235-236

Conklin, Harold C., 26
Conversation, 45, 51, 57, 59, 73-74, 78, 88, 91-92, 105, 117, 151, 155, 164, 169, 172
Corinthian Bar, 151-154
Courtship, 50-51

Dance, 133-134, 202
Das Hofbrau Haus, 73-76
Duncan, Starkey, Jr., 212
Dyads, 60, 71, 73, 77, 97, 105-106, 117, 125, 133-134, 138-139, 155, 160, 169, 172, 183-184, 186, 203, 212

Eastern Orthodox Church, 33, 39, 155-156
El Capitan, 51-56
El Rebozo, 44-50
Emic, 8, 15, 17, 25
Ethnic communities, ix, xii-xiv, 30, 34, 36-37, 101, 130, 232-233
Ethnic group, viii-ix, xi-xiii, 8-9, 29-33, 35-36, 38, 66, 71, 159-160, 162-163, 169, 171, 185, 201, 203, 220, 230, 232
Ethnic identity, viii, xi-xiv, 38, 188
Ethnicity, vii-viii, xi-xiii, 231
Ethnographies, 33, 144
Etic, 8, 10-11, 15-16

Finnerty's Bar, 116-121
Food, 71, 113, 121, 125, 138, 146, 155
French, xii
Freud, S., 12

Gallaher's Bar, 125-129
Geertz, Clifford, 237
Gender, 40-41, 160, 162, 187-188, 202-204, 212, 220, 231, 233
German, xii, 36, 71, 169, 201, 203-204, 220, 230;
   bars, 73-87, 92, 162-163, 166, 168, 170, 172, 185-186, 202, 211, 220-221;
   church, 71, 88-90, 143, 171, 186-188, 202, 211, 221
Goffman, Erving, 2-3, 26-29, 31-32, 35, 52, 60, 183, 231
Gonsaks' Bar, 65-70
Goodenough, Ward H., 18-19, 26
Goodwin, Marjorie H., 212

Greek, 61, 201, 230, 232;
   bar, 146-154, 162-163, 167-170, 172, 185-186, 202, 211, 220;
   church, 71, 155-157, 171, 186-188, 202-203, 211, 220-221

Hall, Edward T., viii, xii, 2-4, 8-10, 14-27, 30-31, 34, 38, 40-42, 57, 73-74, 82-83, 105-106, 144, 156, 159, 162-163, 172, 183-185, 201, 204, 212, 221-222, 230-232, 234, 236-237
Hunter, Albert, xiii

Interior decor, 44, 51, 60-61, 65, 71, 73, 77, 82, 88, 91, 101-102, 104, 116, 121, 125, 133, 138, 151
Irish, 89, 131, 169;
   bars, 116-129, 162-163, 167-168, 170, 172, 186-188, 202, 211, 220;
   churches, 101-103, 163, 186-188, 202, 211, 221;

Jokes, 82-83

Kinesics, 2-5, 7, 10, 39-41, 46, 52-53, 60, 65, 89, 96, 113, 122, 133-134, 138-139, 155, 161-162, 183-201
Kinship, 202
Kruskal-Wallis, 159, 161, 170-172, 180-182, 185, 198-200
Kuhn, Thomas, 2

Labov and Fanshell, 3
Language, xii, 4, 6-7, 17-18, 24-26, 44-45, 51-52, 57, 71, 73, 77, 82, 88, 101, 105, 146-147, 151, 235
Leach, Edmund, 234
Linguistics, 4-14, 18, 25, 38, 231-234, 236
Lithuanian, 117

Mallorca Bar, 138-142
McQuown, 9-10
Men, in bars, 41, 44-46, 50-53, 59-61, 66, 73-74, 77-78, 82-83, 91-92, 96-97, 104-105, 116-117, 121-122, 125, 133-134, 138-139, 146-147, 151;
   in churches, 71, 88-89, 102, 130-131, 144, 187-188, 221
Methodology, ix, 29-43, 230-238

Mexican, 8-9, 61, 143, 169, 220;
  bar, 44-56, 65, 77, 84, 162, 166, 168,
    170, 172, 185-186, 202, 211, 220
  church, 57-58, 113, 171, 186, 202,
    211;
Morris, C. W., 11-14, 23

Newton, Esther, 37-38

Park, Robert E., xiii
Participant observation, ix, 29
Peirce, Charles Sanders, 6-7, 25,
  27-28
Plakos' Bar, 146-150
Polish, 44, 82-83, 170, 220;
  bar, 44, 59-71, 116, 162-163, 166, 168,
    170, 172, 185-186, 202, 211, 220
  church, 44, 71-72, 156, 171, 186-188,
    201, 211-212, 221;
Prejudice, xi
Profanity, 117
Proxemics, xii, 2-29, 31, 34, 38, 45,
  47-52, 71, 159-160, 162, 169, 183,
  201, 221-222, 231-232
Puerto Rican, xii

Rathskeller Bar, 73, 77-81
Red Plume Bar, 133-138
Religion, 44, 235
Ritual, xiv, 7, 32, 38, 51, 164
Roman Catholic Church, 33, 143

Sapir, Edward, 5-6, 8, 13, 26, 230,
  235-237
Schneider, David, xi
Schutz, Alfred, 29
Seating preference, 162-163
Seigal, Sidney, 161
Serbian Club, 104-112
Serbian, 169, 203, 212, 220;
  bar, 104-112, 162-163, 167-168, 170,
    172, 186, 202, 211, 220;
  church, 113-115, 171, 186-188, 201,
    211
Silverstein, Michael, 6-7, 26, 233

Sociofugal, 41, 60, 73, 78, 83, 92,
  105-106, 125, 143-144, 160-161,
  169-182
Sociopetal, 41, 60, 73, 78, 83, 92,
  105-106, 125, 143-144, 160-161,
  169-182
Sommer, R., 187-188, 203
St. Anthony's Church, 155-157
St. Christopher's Church, 130-133
St. Gregory's Church, 113-115
St. Mary's Church, 143-145
St. Nicholaus' Church, 71-72
St. Peter's Church, 88-90
St. Raphael's Church, 101-103
Stanley's Bar, 59-64, 71
Stereotypes, xi-xii, 35, 130, 138
Straussberger Bar, 82-87
Symbol, 13-14, 20, 35, 237

Touching, 40-42, 50-51, 60, 65-66, 71,
  74, 77-78, 89, 91, 97, 102, 106, 113,
  117, 122, 133-134, 138, 144, 147,
  155-156, 186, 201-210, 230
Triads, 60, 91, 106, 143, 146

Vision, 40, 42, 44-45, 60-61, 78, 82-83,
  105-106, 113-114, 146, 151, 169,
  171-172, 211-219
Vocal, 8-9, 40, 42, 51, 91, 117, 121-122,
  130-131, 134, 139, 147, 156, 211,
  220-228

Watson, O. Michael, 7, 9-14, 16, 24, 27,
  31, 40, 159-160, 204, 232
White, Leslie, 23
Whorf, B. L., 17-18
Women, in bars, 40, 50-53, 60-61,
  73-74, 77-78, 83, 91-92, 96-97,
  104, 116-117, 125, 133-134,
  138-139, 146-147, 160, 220-221;
  in church, 71, 88-89, 101-102,
  130-131, 143-144, 155-156, 188,
  202, 221

Young, Chic, 172

31. Barbara L. Reimensnyder. *Powwowing in Union County: A Study of Pennsylvania German Folk Medicine in Context.*
32. Kaoru Oguri Kendis. *A Matter of Comfort: Ethnic Maintenance and Ethnic Style Among Third-Generation Japanese Americans.*
33. Randall Jay Kendis. *An Attitude of Gratitude: The Adaptation to Aging of the Elderly Japanese in America.*
34. Wesley R. Hurt. *Manzano: A Study of Community Disorganization.*
35. Chava Weissler. *Making Judaism Meaningful: Ambivalence and Tradition in a Havurah Community.*
36. Carolyn Stickney Beck. *Our Own Vine and Fig Tree: The persistence of the Mother Bethel Family.*
37. Charles C. Muzny. *The Vietnamese in Oklahoma City: A Study of Ethnic Change.*
38. Sathi Dasgupta. *On the Trail of an Uncertain Dream: Indian Immigrant Experience in America.*
39. Deborah Padgett. *Settlers and Sojourners: A Study of Serbian Adaptation in Milwaukee, Wisconsin.*
40. Margaret S. Boone. *Capital Cubans: Refugee Adaption in Washington, D.C.*
41. George James Patterson, Jr. *The Unassimilated Greeks of Denver.*
42. Mark M. Stolarik. *Immigration and Urbanization: The Slovak Experience.*
43. Dorita Sewell. *Knowing People: A Mexican-American Community's Concept of a person.*
44. M. Ann Walko. *Rejecting the Second Generation Hypothesis: Maintaining Estonian Ethnicity in Lakewood, New Jersey.*
45. Peter D. Goldsmith. *When I Rise Cryin' Holy: Afro-American Denominationalism on the Georgia Coast.*
46. Emily Bradley Massara. *Qué Gordita!: A Study of Weight Among Women in a Puerto Rican Community.*
47. Stephen L. Cabral. *Tradition and Transformation: Portuguese Feasting in New Bedford.*
48. Usha R. Jain. *The Gujaratis of San Francisco.*
49. Aleksandras Gedemintas. *An Interesting Bit of Identity: The Dynamics of Ethnic Identity in a Lithuanian-American Community.*
50. Suzanne J. Terrel. *This Other Kind of Doctors: Traditional Medical Systems in Black Neighborhoods in Austin, Texas.*
51. Annamma Joy. *Ethnicity in Canada: Social Accomodation and Cultural Persistence Among the Sikhs and the Portuguese.*
52. Maria Andrea Miralles. *A Matter of Life and Death: Health-seeking Behavior of Guatemalan Refugees in South Florida.*
53. Greta E. Swenson. *Festivals of Sharing: Family Reunions in America.*
54. Tekle Mariam Woldemikael. *Becoming Black American: Haitians and American Institutions in Evanston, Illinois.*
55. Louis James Cononelos. *In Search of Gold Paved Streets: Greek Immigrant Labor in the Far West, 1900—1920.*
56. Terry J. Prewitt. *German-American Settlement in an Oklahoma Town: Ecologic, Ethnic and Cultural Change.*
57. Myrna Silverman. *Strategies for Social Mobility: Family, Kinship and Ethnicity within Jewish Families in Pittsburgh.*
58. Peter Vasiliadis. *Whose Are You?: Identity and Ethnicity Among the Toronto Macedonians.*
59. Iftikhar Haider Malik. *Pakistanis in Michigan: A Study of Third Culture and Acculturation.*
60. Koozma J. Tarasoff. *Spells, Splits, and Survival in a Russian Canadian Community: A Study of Russian Organizations in the Greater Vancouver Area*
61. Alice H. Reich. *The Cultural Construction of Ethnicity: Chicanos in the University.*
62. Greta Kwik. *The Indos in Southern California.*
63. Laurence Marshall Carucci, et al. *Shared Spaces: Contexts of Interaction in Chicago's Ethnic Communities.*
64. Francis W. Chapin. *Tides of Migration: A Study of Migration Decision-Making and Social Progress in São Miguel, Azores.*
65. Robert B. Klymasz. *The Ukrainian Folk Ballad in Canada. With Musical Transcriptions by Kenneth Peacock.*
66. Elaine H. Maas. *The Jews of Houston: An Ethnographic Study.*
67. James W. Kiriazis. *Children of the Colossus: The Rhodian Greek Immigrants in the United States.*